# THE FATHERS
OF THE CHURCH

A NEW TRANSLATION

VOLUME 144

# THE FATHERS OF THE CHURCH

A NEW TRANSLATION

# CASSIODORUS, ST. GREGORY THE GREAT, AND ANONYMOUS GREEK SCHOLIA

## WRITINGS ON THE APOCALYPSE

*Translated by*

FRANCIS X. GUMERLOCK,
MARK DELCOGLIANO, AND T. C. SCHMIDT

THE CATHOLIC UNIVERSITY OF AMERICA PRESS
Washington, D.C.

LIBRARY OF CONGRESS CATALOGING-IN-PUBLICATION DATA

*Names:* Cassiodorus, Senator, approximately 487–approximately
580, author. | Gregory I, Pope, approximately 540–604, author. |
Gumerlock, Francis X., translator. | DelCogliano, Mark, translator.
| Schmidt, T. C. (Thomas C.), translator.

*Title:* Writings on the apocalypse / Cassiodorus, St. Gregory the
Great, and anonymous Greek scholia ; translated by Francis X.
Gumerlock, Mark DelCogliano, and T. C. Schmidt.

*Identifiers:* LCCN 2021062209 | ISBN 9780813234915 (cloth) |
ISBN 9780813234922 (ebook)

*Subjects:* LCSH: Apocalyptic literature. | Bible. Revelation—
Criticism, interpretation, etc.

*Classification:* LCC BS646 .W7513 2022 | DDC 228/.06—dc23/
eng/20220222

LC record available at https://lccn.loc.gov/2021062209

# CONTENTS

# ABBREVIATIONS

ACW  Ancient Christian Writers (New York)

CCSL  Corpus Christianorum, Series Latina (Turnhout)

CSEL  Corpus Scriptorum Ecclesiasticorum Latinorum (Vienna)

FC  The Fathers of the Church (Washington, DC)

*OTP*  *Old Testament Pseudepigrapha*, ed. Charlesworth (New York)

PL  Patrologiae Cursus Completus, Series Latina (Paris)

SC  Sources Chrétiennes (Paris)

*TLG*  *Thesaurus Linguae Graecae* (Oxford)

# SELECT BIBLIOGRAPHY

### Editions of Primary Sources

*Cassiodori Senatoris Complexiones in Apocalypsi.* Edited by Roger Gryson. Corpus Christianorum, Series Latina 107. Turnhout: Brepols, 2003; PL 70:1405–1418.

*Cassiodori Senatoris Institutiones.* Edited by R.A. B. Mynors. Oxford: Clarendon, 1961; PL 70:1105–1220.

*De testimoniis in Apocalypsin S. Joannis Apostoli.* PL 79:1107–1122.

*Grégoire le Grand. Règle pastorale.* Edited by Bruno Judic, Floribert Rommel, and Charles Morel. SC 381 & 382. Paris: Cerf, 1992.

*S. Gregorii Magni Moralia in Iob.* Edited by Marcus Adriaen. CCSL 143, 143A, and 143B. Turnhout: Brepols, 1979–1985.

*Gregorius Magnus. Homiliae in Evangelia.* Edited by Raymond Étaix. CCSL 141. Turnhout: Brepols, 1999.

*Magni Aurelii Cassiodori Senatoris opera,* Pars II, 4. Edited by Roger Gryson. CCSL 98B. Turnhout: Brepols, 2016.

*Sancti Gregorii Magni Homiliae in Hiezechihelem prophetem.* Edited by Marcus Adriaen. CCSL 142. Turnhout: Brepols, 1971.

*Scholia in Apocalypsin.* Edited by Panayiotis Tzamalikos. *An Ancient Commentary on the Book of Revelation: A Critical Edition of the Scholia in Apocalypsin.* New York: Cambridge University Press, 2013.

———. Edited by C. H. Turner. "Origen Scholia in Apocalypsin." *The Journal of Theological Studies* 25, no. 97 (1923): 1–16. https://doi.org/10.1093/jts/os-XXV.97.1.

———. Edited by C. H. Turner. "The Text of the Newly Discovered Scholia of Origen on the Apocalypse." *The Journal of Theological Studies* 13, no. 51 (1912): 386–97. https://doi.org/10.1093/jts/os-XIII.51.386.

———. Edited by Constantin Diobouniotis and Adolf Harnack. "Der Scholien-Kommentar des Origenes zur Apokalypse Johannis nebst einem Stück aus Irenaeus, lib. V, Graece entdeckt und herausgegeben." *Texte und Untersuchungen* 38.3 (1911): 1–88.

### Translations of Primary Sources

*Cassiodorus: Institutions of Divine and Secular Learning and On the Soul.* Translated by James W. Halporn with an introduction by Mark Vessey. Translated Texts for Historians 42. Liverpool: Liverpool University Press, 2004.

Courreau, Joël, and Adalbert-Gautier Hamman, eds. *L'Apocalypse expliquée par Césaire d'Arles. Scholies attribuées à Origène.* Translated by Solange Bouquet. Paris: Desclée de Brouwer, 1989.

*Gregory the Great. Forty Gospel Homilies.* Translated by David Hurst. Cistercian Studies Series 123. Kalamazoo, MI: Cistercian, 1990.

*Gregory the Great. Morals on the Book of Job.* 4 vols. Library of the Fathers of the Holy Catholic Church 18, 21, 23, and 31. Oxford: J. H. Parker, 1844–1850.

*Gregory the Great. Moral Reflections on the Book of Job.* 6 vols. Translated by Brian Kerns. Cistercian Studies Series 249, 257, 258, 259, 260, 261. Collegeville, MN: Liturgical Press, 2014–2022.

*The Homilies of Saint Gregory the Great on the Book of the Prophet Ezekiel.* Translated by Theodosia Grey. Etna, CA: Center for Traditionalist Orthodox Studies, 1990.

*An Introduction to Divine and Human Readings by Cassiodorus.* Translation with an introduction and notes by Leslie Webber Jones. New York: Columbia University Press, 1946.

Müller, Darius, and Edmund Gerke. "Eine deutsche Übersetzung der Scholia in Apocalypsin mit Einleitung." In *Studien zum Text der Apokalypse II,* edited by Marcus Sigismund and Darius Müller, 477–520. Arbeiten zur neutestamentlichen Textforschung 50. Berlin: De Gruyter, 2017. https://doi.org/10.1515/9783110558784.

*St. Gregory the Great. The Book of Pastoral Rule.* Translated by George E. Demacopoulos. Popular Patristics Series 34. Crestwood, NY: St. Vladimir's Seminary Press, 2007.

*St. Gregory the Great. Pastoral Care.* Translated by Henry Davis. ACW 11. Mahwah, NJ: Newman, 1950.

Tzamalikos, Panayiotis. *An Ancient Commentary on the Book of Revelation: A Critical Edition of the Scholia in Apocalypsin.* New York: Cambridge University Press, 2013.

### Other Ancient Texts: Editions and Translations

Ambrose Autpert. *Ambrosii Autperti opera.* Edited by Robert Weber. Corpus Christianorum Continuatio Mediaevalis 27 & 27A. Turnhout: Brepols, 1975.

Andrew of Caesarea. *Commentary on the Apocalypse.* Translated by Eugenia Scarvelis Constantinou. FC 123. Washington, DC: The Catholic University of America Press, 2011.

Augustine. *The City of God by Saint Augustine.* Translated by Marcus Dods. New York: Random House, 1950.

Cassiodorus. *Explanation of the Psalms.* 3 vols. Translated by P. G. Walsh. ACW 51, 52, 53. Mahwah, NJ: Paulist Press, 1990.

———. *Magni Aurelii Cassiodori variarum libri XII.* Edited by A. J. Fridh. CCSL 96. Turnhout: Brepols, 1973.

———. *Cassiodorus' Variae: A Complete and Annotated Translation.* Translated by M. Shane Bjornlie. Oakland: University of California Press, 2019.

Didymus the Blind. *Commentary on Zechariah.* Translated by Robert C. Hill. FC 111. Washington, DC: The Catholic University of America Press, 2013.

———. *Didyme l'Aveugle: Sur la Genèse.* Edited by Pierre Nautin. SC 233, 244 (vol. 1–2). Paris: Cerf, 1977.

————. *Didyme l'Aveugle: Sur Zacharie*. Edited by Louis Doutreleau. SC 83, 84, 85. Paris: Cerf, 1962.

Gregory the Great. *Grégoire le Grand. Commentaire sur le Cantique des Cantiques*. Edited by Rodrigue Bélanger. SC 314. Paris: Cerf, 1984.

————. *Grégoire le Grand. Dialogues*. Edited by Adalbert de Vogüé and Paul Antin. SC 251, 260, and 265. Paris: Cerf, 1978–1980.

————. *Gregory the Great on the Song of Songs*. Translation and introduction by Mark DelCogliano. Cistercian Studies Series 244. Collegeville, MN: Liturgical Press, 2012.

————. *The Letters of Gregory the Great*. Translated by John R. C. Martyn. Medieval Sources in Translation 40. Toronto: Pontifical Institute of Mediaeval Studies, 2004.

————. *S. Gregorii Magni Registrum epistularum*. Edited by Dag Norberg. CCSL 140 & 140A. Turnhout: Brepols, 1982.

————. *Sancti Gregorii Magni Expositiones in Canticum Canticorum, in Librum Primum Regum*. Edited by Patrick Verbraken. CCSL 144. Turnhout: Brepols, 1963.

————. *St. Gregory the Great: Dialogues*. Translated by Odo Zimmerman. FC 39. New York: Fathers of the Church, 1959.

Gryson, Roger, ed. *Commentaria minora in Apocalypsin Johannis*. CCSL 107. Turnhout: Brepols, 2003.

Gumerlock, Francis X., ed. *Early Latin Commentaries on the Apocalypse*. Kalamazoo, MI: Medieval Institute Publications, 2016.

Hippolytus of Rome. *Hippolyte de Rome sur les bénédictions d'Isaac, de Jacob et de Moïse*. Edited by Maurice Brière, Louis Mariès, and B.-Ch. Mercier. Patrologia Orientalis 27.1–2. Paris: Firmin-Didot, 1957.

Jerome. *Commentary on Isaiah; Origen Homilies 1–9 on Isaiah*. Translated by Thomas P. Scheck. ACW 68. New York: Paulist Press, 2015.

Oecumenius. *Commentary on the Apocalypse*. Translated by John N. Suggit. FC 112. Washington, DC: The Catholic University of America Press, 2006.

Origen. *Commentary on the Epistle to the Romans, Books 1–5*. Translated by Thomas P. Scheck. FC 105. Washington, DC: The Catholic University of America Press, 2009.

————. *Commentary on the Gospel According to John: Books 1–10*. Translated by Ronald E. Heine. FC 80. Washington, DC: The Catholic University of America Press, 1989.

————. *Homilies 1–14 on Ezekiel*. Translated by Thomas P. Scheck. ACW 62. New York: Paulist Press, 2010.

————. *Origen on First Principles: Being Koetschau's Text of the De Principiis*. Translated by George William Butterworth. London: Society for the Promotion of Christian Knowledge, 1936.

————. *Origenes. Contra Celsum libri VIII*. Edited by Miroslav Marcovich. Leiden: Brill, 2001.

————. *Origenes Werke: Commentarius in Mattheaum*. Edited by Erich Klostermann. Die Griechischen Christlichen Schriftsteller 38.2. Leipzig: J. C. Hinrichs, 1899.

Primasius. *Primasius episcopus Hadrumetinus. Commentarius in Apocalypsin*. Edited by A. W. Adams. CCSL 92. Turnhout: Brepols, 1985.

Tyconius. *Tyconii Afri Expositio Apocalypseos.* Edited by Roger Gryson. CCSL 107A. Turnhout: Brepols, 2011.

———. *Exposition of the Apocalypse.* Translated by Francis X. Gumerlock. Introduction and notes by David C. Robinson. FC 134. Washington, DC: The Catholic University of America Press, 2017.

Victorinus of Pettau. *Victorini episcopi Petavionensis opera.* Edited by Iohannes Haussleiter. CSEL 49. Vienna: Tempsky, 1916.

———. *Victorinus Poetovionensis. Opera quae supersunt.* Edited by Roger Gryson. CCSL 5. Turnhout: Brepols, 2017.

Weinrich, William, trans. *Greek Commentaries on Revelation.* Downers Grove, IL: InterVarsity, 2011.

———. *Latin Commentaries on Revelation.* Downers Grove, IL: InterVarsity, 2011.

*Modern Sources*

Allen, Garrick. "Review of *An Ancient Commentary on the Book of Revelation: A Critical Edition of the Scholia in Apocalypsin* by P. Tzamalikos." *The Two Cities* (blog), October 4, 2014. http://www.thetwocities.com/book-reviews/review-of-an-ancient -commentary-on-the-book-of-revelation-a-critical-edition-of-the-scholia-in -apocalypsin-by-p-tzamalikos/.

———. "The Reception of Scripture and Exegetical Resources in the Scholia in Apocalypsin (GA 2351)." In *Commentaries, Catenae and Biblical Tradition*, edited by H. A. G. Houghton, 141–63. Piscataway, NJ: Gorgias Press, 2016.

Amirav, Hagit, Emmanouela Grypeou, and Guy Stroumsa, eds. *Apocalypticism and Eschatology in Late Antiquity: Encounters in the Abrahamic Religions, 6th–8th Centuries.* Dudley, MA: Peeters, 2017.

Auwers, Jean-Marie. "An Ancient Commentary on the Book of Revelation: A Critical Edition of the Scholia in Apocalypsin." *Ephemerides Theologicae Lovanienses* 90:4 (2014): 781.

Bammel, Caroline P. "A New Witness to the Scholia from Origen in the Codex von der Goltz." In *Origeniana Quinta: Papers of the 5th International Origen Congress, Boston College, 14–18 August 1989*, edited by Robert J. Daly, 137–41. Louvain: University Press, 1992.

Barnish, Samuel, Lellia Cracco Ruggini, Luciana Cuppo, Ronald Marchese, and Marlene Breu. *Vivarium in Context.* Vicenza: Pozzo, 2008.

Bjornlie, M. Shane. *Politics and Tradition between Rome, Ravenna, and Constantinople: A Study of Cassiodorus and the* Variae, *527–554.* New York: Cambridge University Press, 2013.

Boysson, A. de. "Avons-nous un commentaire d'Origène sur l'Apocalypse?" *Revue Biblique (1892–1940)* 10:4 (1913): 555–67.

Cardini, Franco. *Cassiodorus the Great. Rome, Barbarians and Monasticism.* Milan: Jaca, 2009.

Csaki, Luciana Cuppo. "The Monastery of Cassiodorus Vivariense: Reconnaissance and Research, 1994–1999." In *Frühes Christentum zwischen Rom und Konstantinopel*, edited by R. Harreither, Ph. Pergola, R. Pillinger, A. Pulz, 301–16. Vatican City: Pontificio Istituto di Archeologia Cristiana, 2006.

Daley, Brian E. *The Hope of the Early Church: A Handbook of Patristic Eschatology.* Grand Rapids, MI: Baker, 1991.

Daly, Robert J., ed. *Apocalyptic Thought in Early Christianity.* Grand Rapids, MI: Baker, 2009.

Demacopoulos, George E. *Gregory the Great: Ascetic, Pastor, and First Man of Rome.* South Bend, IN: University of Notre Dame Press, 2015.

Diekamp, Franz. "Diobouniotis, Constantin, und Adolf Harnack, Der Scholien-Kommentar des Origenes zur Apokalypse Johannis." *Theologische Revue* 11:2 (1912): 51–55.

Diobouniotis, Constantin, and Nikos Athanasion Beēs. "Hippolyts Schrift Über Die Segnungen Jakobs." *Texte und Untersuchungen* 38:1 (1911): 1–60.

Elliott, J. K. "Manuscripts of the Book of Revelation Collated by H. C. Hoskier." *The Journal of Theological Studies* 40:1 (1989): 100–111. https://doi.org/10.1093/jts/40.1.100.

Emmerson, Richard K., and Bernard McGinn. *The Apocalypse in the Middle Ages.* Ithaca, NY: Cornell University Press, 1992.

Étaix, Raymond. "Le *Liber testimoniorum* de Paterius." *Revue des Sciences Religieuses* 32 (1958): 66–78.

———. "Les commentaires patristiques latins de l'Apocalypse," *Revue théologique de Louvain* 28 (1997): 305–37.

———. *Vetus Latina: Die Reste der altlateinischen Bibel*, 26/2. Apocalypsis Johannis. Freiburg: Herder, 2000–2003.

Gumerlock, Francis X. "Patristic Commentaries on Revelation: An Update." *Kerux* 27:3 (2012): 37–43.

Hester, Kevin L. *Eschatology and Pain in St. Gregory the Great: The Christological Synthesis of Gregory's Morals on the Book of Job.* Eugene, OR: Wipf & Stock, 2008.

Heydemann, Gerda. "Biblical Israel and the Christian *gentes.* Social metaphors and concepts of community in Cassiodorus's *Expositio psalmorum.*" In *Strategies of Identification. Early Medieval Perspectives*, edited by Walter Pohl and Gerda Heydemann, 98–141. Turnhout: Brepols, 2013.

Hoskier, Herman Charles. *Concerning the Text of the Apocalypse.* 2 vols. London: B. Quaritch, Ltd., 1929. https//catalog.hathitrust.org/Record/001411390.

Huber, Konrad. "An Ancient Commentary on the Book of Revelation: A Critical Edition of the *Scholia in Apocalypsin.*" *The Journal of Theological Studies* 66:2 (2015): 798–800. https://doi.org/10.1093/jts/flv035.

Johnson, David W. "Purging the Poison: The Revision of Pelagius' Pauline Commentaries by Cassiodorus and his Students." Dissertation. Princeton, NJ: Princeton Theological Seminary, 1989.

Junod, Eric. "À propos des soi-disant scolies sur l'Apocalypse d'Origène." *Rivista di storia e letteratura religiosa* 20 (1984): 112–21.

Kavrus-Hoffmann, Nadezhda. "Catalogue of Greek Medieval and Renaissance Manuscripts in the Collections of the United States of America, Part V.1: Harvard University, The Houghton Library." *Manuscripta* 54:1 (2010): 64–139. https://doi.org/10.1484/J.MSS.1.100788.

Kelly, Joseph F. T. "Early Medieval Evidence for Twelve Homilies by Origen on the Apocalypse." *Vigiliae Christianae* 39:3 (1985): 273–79. https://doi.org/10.2307/1583857.

Klostermann, Erich. "Der Scholien-Kommentar des Origenes zur Apokalypse Johannis." *Theologische Literaturzeitung* 27:3 (1912): 73–74.

McGinn, Bernard. "Exegesis of the Apocalypse in Latin Christianity." In *The Calabrian Abbot: Joachim of Fiore in the History of Western Thought*, edited by Bernard McGinn, 74–97. New York: Macmillan, 1985.

———. "Turning Points in Early Christian Apocalypse Exegesis." In *Apocalyptic Thought in Early Christianity*, edited by Robert J. Daly, 81–105. Grand Rapids, MI: Baker, 2009.

Nautin, Pierre. *Origène: Sa vie et son œuvre*. Paris: Beauchesne, 1977.

O'Donnell, James J. *Cassiodorus*. Berkeley: University of California Press, 1979.

Palmer, James T. *The Apocalypse in the Early Middle Ages*. New York: Cambridge University Press, 2014.

Parker, David C. "An Ancient Commentary on the Book of Revelation. A Critical Edition of the 'Scholia in Apocalypsin'. By P. Tzamalikos." *The Journal of Ecclesiastical History* 66:2 (2015): 391–93. https://doi.org/10.1017/S0022046914002723.

Plaxco, Kellen. "An Ancient Commentary on the Book of Revelation: A Critical Edition of the *Scholia in Apocalypsin*. Translated and edited by Panagiotes Tzamalikos." *Theological Studies* 75:4 (2014): 903–5. https://doi.org/10.1177/0040563914548658c.

Poole, Kevin. "The Western Apocalypse Commentary Tradition of the Early Middle Ages." In *A Companion to the Premodern Apocalypse*, edited by Michael A. Ryan, 103–43. Leiden: Brill, 2016.

Ramelli, Ilaria. "Origen's Interpretation of Violence in the Apocalypse." In *Ancient Christian Interpretations of "Violent Texts" in the Apocalypse*, edited by Andreas Merkt, Tobias Nicklas, and Joseph Verheyden, 1st ed., 46–62. Göttingen: Vandenhoeck & Ruprecht, 2011. Novum Testamentum et Orbis Antiquus/Studien zur Umwelt des Neuen Testaments 92. Vandenhoeck & Ruprecht, 2011. https://doi.org/10.13109/9783666539763.46.

———. "Origen's Anti-Subordinationism and its Heritage in the Nicene and Cappadocian Line." *Vigiliae Christianae* 65:1 (2011): 21–49.

Rapisarda lo Menzo, Grazia. "Gregorio Magno e l'Apocalypse." *Orpheus* 6 (1985): 449–67.

Recchia, Vincenzo. *L'esegesi di Gregorio Magno al Cantico dei Cantici*. Turin: Società Editrice Internationale, 1967.

Richard, M. "Une scolie d'Origène indûment attribuée à Denys d'Alexandrie." *Revue d'Histoire Ecclésiastique* 33:1 (1937): 44.

Robinson, J. Armitage. "Origen's Comments on the Apocalypse." *The Journal of Theological Studies* 13, no. 50 (1912): 295–97.

Ryan, Michael A., ed. *A Companion to the Premodern Apocalypse*. Leiden: Brill, 2016.

Schermann, Theod. "Ein Scholienkommentar des Origenes?" *Theologische Revue* 11:1 (1912): 29.

Schmidt, T. C. *The Book of Revelation and Its Eastern Commentators: Making the New Testament in the Early Christian World*. Cambridge, UK: Cambridge University Press, 2021.

Shoemaker, Stephen. "The Afterlife of the Apocalypse of John in Byzantine Apocalyptic Literature and Commentary." In *The New Testament in Byzantium*, edited by Derek Krueger and Robert Nelson, 301–16. Washington, DC: Dumbarton Oaks, 2016.

Skard, Eiliv. "Zum Scholien-kommentar des Origenes zur Apokalypse Johannis." *Symbolae Osloenses* 15:1 (1936): 204–8.

Stählin, Otto. "Der Scholien-Kommentar des Origenes zur Apokalypse Johannis." *Berliner philologische wochenschrift* 32:5 (1912): 132–40.

Steinhauser, Kenneth B. *The Apocalypse Commentary of Tyconius: A History of Its Reception and Influence.* New York: Peter Lang, 1987.

Strathmann, D. "Origenes und die Johannesoffenbarung." *Neue Kirchliche Zeitschrift* 34 (1923): 228–36.

Troncarelli, Franco. *Vivarium. The Books, the Fate.* Turnhout: Brepols, 1998.

Tzamalikos, Panayiotis. *A Newly Discovered Greek Father: Cassian the Sabaite Eclipsed by John Cassian of Marseilles.* Leiden: Brill, 2012.

———. *Origen: Cosmology and Ontology of Time.* Leiden: Brill, 2006.

———. *Origen: Philosophy of History & Eschatology.* Leiden: Brill, 2007.

———. *The Real Cassian Revisited: Monastic Life, Greek Paideia, and Origenism in the Sixth Century.* Leiden: Brill, 2012.

Vukovic, Marijana. "The Library of Vivarium: Cassiodorus and the Classics." Master's thesis. Budapest: Central European University, 2007.

Wilmart, André. "Le recueil grégorien de Paterius et les fragments wisigothiques de Paris." *Revue Bénédictine* 39 (1927): 81–104.

Wohlenberg, Gustav. "Ein neuaufgefundener Kodex der Offenbarung Johannis nebst alten Erläuterungen." *Theologisches Literaturblatt* 33:2 (1912): 25–30.

———. "(Part 2) Ein neuaufgefundener Kodex der Offenbarung Johannis nebst alten Erläuterungen." *Theologisches Literaturblatt* 33:3 (1912): 49–57.

———. "Noch einiges zu dem Scholienkommentar (des Origenes) zur Offenbarung Johannis." *Theologisches Literaturblatt* 33:10 (1912): 217–20.

Young, Frances. *Biblical Exegesis and the Formation of Christian Culture.* Cambridge: Cambridge University Press, 1997.

# PREFACE

In recent years most of the extant patristic commentaries on the Apocalypse have been translated into English. Exegesis on the Apocalypse in other genres, however, has not received much attention. This material may be found in biblical prefaces, poems, homilies, apocalyptic literature, and tracts on the Antichrist. This volume contains three treatises on the Apocalypse in genres different from the traditional "commentary." The first is an introduction to and summary of the Apocalypse by Cassiodorus (d. 580). The second is a collection of fifty-five excerpts on the Apocalypse gathered from various writings of Gregory the Great (d. 604). The third text consists of thirty-eight scholia, brief remarks made on passages of the Apocalypse, which were gathered from a variety of Greek patristic authors but collected in a single text.

All three of these writings contain valuable insights concerning patristic interpretations of the Apocalypse. *Brief Explanations on the Apocalypse* by Cassiodorus, translated by myself, was written in Latin at the Vivarium, a monastery in southern Italy. It provides a summary of the entire Apocalypse. In it Cassiodorus wonderfully synthesizes the eschatological reading of the Apocalypse promulgated by Victorinus of Petovium (c. 260) and the ecclesiastical reading of Tyconius of Carthage (c. 380). The *Testimonies of Gregory the Great on the Apocalypse* show that Gregory approached the Apocalypse mainly with a grammatical exegetical method, but also gave symbolic interpretations of many passages in the Apocalypse. In addition, he engaged with statements in the Apocalypse to answer apparent biblical contradictions, reinforce doctrinal orthodoxy, and encourage his readers in holy living. Mark DelCogliano, an excellent scholar who previously translated Gregory's *Commentary on the Song of Songs*, provides the introduction to and the translation of that collection. The anonymous collection of Greek *Scholia on the Apocalypse* from the

fourth or fifth century offers allegorical interpretations of the Apocalypse consistent with the exegetical methods of certain early Alexandrian writers. The *Scholia* also show that Greek patristic writers
had used the Apocalypse to defend Nicene Christology. Thomas
(T. C.) Schmidt, who previously translated Hippolytus's *Commentary
on Daniel* and *Chronicon* from Greek into English, provides a lucid
translation of the *Scholia* and a thorough introduction, which at
times challenges previous scholarship on that text and shows the
difficulty of determining its authorship with certainty.

These texts provide an understanding of what early Christians
thought about the Apocalypse that is more comprehensive than that
furnished by the traditional commentaries, as all display unique
patristic interpretations of the Apocalypse. In addition, these three
treatises are sure to stimulate research on the history of the interpretation of the Apocalypse. For example, in the first half of the
sixth century, Tyconius's *Exposition of the Apocalypse* exerted a strong
influence on the homilies on the Apocalypse by Caesarius of Arles
and on the commentary on the same by Primasius; but in the latter
half of the sixth century, at least in the writings of Cassiodorus and
Gregory, the influence of Tyconius is far less. What factors might
explain the diminishing influence of Tyconius later in that century?
Was Gregory influenced at all by Tyconius's interpretations, and if
so, on which particular passages of the Apocalypse? Since both Cassiodorus and Gregory spent considerable time in Constantinople,
do their writings on the Apocalypse reveal any influence of Eastern
interpretive traditions? Do their interpretations of the Apocalypse
bear any similarity to the material in the Greek *Scholia*, and if so,
were there sources common to all three? What is the relationship, if
any, of the Greek *Scholia* translated in this volume to the Greek commentaries on the Apocalypse of Oecumenius and Andrew? These
three treatises may provide answers to such questions. At the very
least, these texts are windows through which a reader may view how
these specific patristic authors, all of whom regarded the Apocalypse as a revelation from the Son of God, explained its difficult passages and used that revelation to teach their respective audiences.

Francis X. Gumerlock
Westminster, Colorado
November 4, 2019

# CASSIODORUS
## *BRIEF EXPLANATIONS ON THE APOCALYPSE*

*Translated by*

FRANCIS X. GUMERLOCK

# INTRODUCTION

## CASSIODORUS, *BRIEF EXPLANATIONS* *ON THE APOCALYPSE*

*Author and Date.* Flavius Magnus Aurelius Cassiodorus Senator was born into a noble Christian family in southern Italy about 485, and served as a statesman in the Ostrogothic kingdom—as quaestor in 507, consul in 514, master of offices in 523 succeeding the executed Boethius, and praetorian prefect in 533. About 537 or 538, he retired from political life and focused his energies on study and writing on theological and scriptural subjects. About 540 he moved from Ravenna to Constantinople, where he wrote a large commentary on the Psalms. Then about 554 he returned to Italy and lived near the Vivarium, a monastery he had founded earlier on his family estate near Scyllaceum in Calabria. There he labored in scholarly pursuits in community with other Christian scholar-monks until his death in 580.[1]

During his residence near Vivarium, Cassiodorus wrote *Complexiones*, which are brief explanations on the Pauline epistles, the Acts of the Apostles, and the Apocalypse.[2] He wrote those on the

---

1. M. Shane Bjornlie, *Cassiodorus' Variae: A Complete and Annotated Translation* (Oakland: University of California Press, 2019); M. L. Angisani Sanfilippo, "Cassiodorus, Flavius Magnus Aurelius," in *Encyclopedia of Ancient Christianity*, Vol. 1, ed. Angelo Di Berardino, 440–42 (Downers Grove, IL: InterVarsity, 2014); M. Shane Bjornlie, *Politics and Tradition Between Rome, Ravenna and Constantinople: A Study of Cassiodorus and the* Variae, *527–554* (New York: Cambridge University Press, 2013); Andrew Scheil, "Cassiodorus, Flavius Magnus Aurelius," in Jana K. Schulman, ed., *The Rise of the Medieval World, 500–1300: A Biographical Dictionary* (Westport, CT: Greenwood, 2002); 94–96; W. Bürsgens, "Cassiodorus," in *Dictionary of Early Christian Literature*, ed. Siegmar Döpp and Wilhelm Geerlings, 117–19 (New York: Crossroad, 2000).

2. In his *Complexiones in Epistulis Apostolorum* (PL 70: 1321) Cassiodorus characterized the *complexiones* as brief explanations that do not discuss every word but

Apocalypse about 580 when very advanced in age.[3] This text, which I have entitled *Brief Explanations on the Apocalypse*, survived in only one manuscript, dated to the end of the sixth or beginning of the seventh century. It was discovered in 1712 by Scipio Maffei and is preserved in a library in Verona.[4] The editions in PL 70: 1405–18 and of Roger Gryson in his *Commentaria minora in Apocalypsin Johannis* in CCSL 107: 113–29 were used for the present translation.

*Purpose and Method.* In his prologue, Cassiodorus states that the design of his work is merely to introduce the Apocalypse of John to his readers. He laments that at present he cannot explain its obscure mysteries more thoroughly, as they should be explained, but states that Tyconius did this; and even though Tyconius was a Donatist, God uses his work in a way similar to that in which a doctor makes an antidote out of poison.

Cassiodorus's method is to divide the Apocalypse into thirty-three sections corresponding to the age of Jesus. He begins each section with a quotation from the Apocalypse and then summarizes the contents of that section, closely following the biblical text. In the translation, Cassiodorus's enumeration of sections has been retained, and the biblical quotation that begins each section has been placed in italics. For convenience and reference, the modern division of chapters in the Book of Revelation has been added, along with verse numbers corresponding to Cassiodorus's explanations. Other biblical quotations of more than four or five words in length are placed in quotation marks.

---

provide a summary. For more on the term *complexio* in Cassiodorus, see Kevin Poole, "The Western Apocalypse Commentary Tradition of the Early Middle Ages," in *A Companion to the Premodern Apocalypse*, ed. Michael A. Ryan, 103–43 at 114–15 (Boston: Brill, 2016); and Mark Stansbury, "Early-Medieval Biblical Commentaries, Their Writers and Readers," *Frühmittelalterliche Studien* 33 (1999): 49–92 at 66.

3. In the preface to Cassiodorus's treatise on orthography, where he says he is writing at age 93, he lists as a work written shortly before that one "a very brief explanation" of the Apocalypse; PL 70: 1241. Roger Gryson's introduction to the critical edition of the *Complexiones in Apocalypsi* (in *Commentaria minora*, CCSL 107: 101) dates the text to about 580, as does A. J. Fridh, ed., *Magni Aurelii Cassiodori variarum libri XII*, CCSL 96: xi.

4. James J. O'Donnell, *Cassiodorus* (Berkeley: University of California Press, 1979), 225.

Cassiodorus believed that John wrote in figures, mysteries, and allegories.[5] Unfortunately he does not explain many of the Apocalypse's mysteries. For example, Cassiodorus says on Rv 6.12 that when John wrote about the occurrence of an earthquake, he was speaking "through allegory"; but he never explains the allegory.[6] Similarly, he wrote that the appearance of the locusts in Rv 9.10 "is described in a mystery," that a passage in Rv 12 "contains great mystery," and that the distance of one thousand six hundred stadia in Rv 14.15 has "mystical significance," but explains none of these. Cassiodorus's *Brief Explanations* also does not explain the mysterious number of the beast in Rv 13.18 or the identity of Gog and Magog in Rv 20.8. According to the prologue, Cassiodorus's work was only meant as an introduction to the Apocalypse. Because of this, he fears that some may criticize the work because it omits the meaning of the visions. Nevertheless, he believes that a diligent reader can still find benefit from it. Although most of the work simply summarizes the biblical text,[7] nevertheless some of his interpretations of the Apocalypse can be gleaned in his *Brief Explanations*.

*Eschatology.* From the beginning of the work, Cassiodorus states that the Apocalypse is "about the end of the world."[8] He sees the Second Coming of Christ for judgment throughout the Apocalypse, in passages like Rv 1.7; 2.16; 3.3, 11–12; 14.6, 14; 19.11–15; and 22.12. In light of Christ's majesty and power displayed in the Second Coming, he says that "the generation at the end of the world" should fear because of their sins.[9] The defeat of the Antichrist, the event of the general resurrection, and the arrival of the heavenly kingdom will take place at that time.[10] Some people, however,

5. On Rv 6.12; 9.10; 12.6; 14.19; 19.18; 20.2; 21.12–18.
6. Tyconius (*Exposition of the Apocalypse*, on Rv 6.12; CCSL 107A: 142. FC 134: 78) saw the earthquake as symbolic of the final persecution.
7. As Kenneth B. Steinhauser observed, the *Complexiones* "was an abstract of the book of the Apocalypse serving as a brief introduction for students"; *The Apocalypse Commentary of Tyconius: A History of Its Reception and Influence* (New York: Peter Lang, 1987), 98.
8. On Rv 1.1.
9. On Rv 14.14.
10. On Rv 2.28; 11.15; 17.14; 20.6, 12–15; 21.3–4, 7.

will be excluded from that kingdom and will suffer eternal punishment.[11]

Before the Second Coming, certain events "predicted to happen at the end of the world" will take place.[12] One is the darkening of the sun and moon.[13] Another is the appearance of Enoch, Elijah, and the Antichrist "reserved for the end of the world."[14] Identified as the *false prophet* of Rv 19.20 and 20.10, the Antichrist will make war against the saints for three and a half years. He will perform many miraculous signs, speak blasphemous things against God, and make an idol that will be "worshiped with great devotion."[15] There is no hint in Cassiodorus's *Brief Explanations* that he believed the events of the end were imminent, and he indicates no parallel correspondence between specific political events, religious upheavals, or natural disasters in his own lifetime and those described in the visions in the Apocalypse. The world, he explains, is indeed worn out from various conflicts,[16] but the exact timing of its end "is altogether unknown."[17]

*Interpretations in his Summary.* Although Cassiodorus's text is a summary, nevertheless his interpretive comments are interspersed throughout. On Rv 1.1 Cassiodorus gives reasons why the Apocalypse was revealed. It was so that the devout might gain confidence and unbelievers might fear. He interprets the *seven spirits* in Rv 1.4 and 4.5 as seven angels. A more common interpretation of the seven spirits in late Western antiquity was that they signified the one Holy Spirit, who is sevenfold in his operation.[18] For his interpretation of the seven spirits as angels, Cassiodorus may have associated the phrase *seven spirits before his throne* in Rv 1.4 with *seven angels before the throne* in Rv 8.2. On this he was also influenced by Tobit 12.15,

11. On Rv 2.16; 21.8; 22.15.
12. On Rv 6.13–17.
13. On Rv 6.12.
14. On Rv 11.3; 17.12.
15. On Rv 13.1–6, 11–17.
16. On Rv 3.8.
17. On Rv 20.1, 7.
18. This was based on Is 11.2. Victorinus, *Commentary on the Apocalypse*, on Rv 1.4; Primasius, *Commentary on the Apocalypse*, on Rv 1.4; 4.5.

which mentions seven angels in the presence of the Lord.[19] Such interpretation of the seven spirits as angels by Cassiodorus was an iteration of a Greek exegetical tradition.[20] This is not surprising; for, before writing the *Brief Explanations* Cassiodorus had resided in Constantinople for over a decade.

The descriptions of Christ in Rv 1 point to his divinity, although Cassiodorus claims that John, being human, did not see the full essence of the divine nature, which will only be revealed to humans after the resurrection. Throughout the *Brief Explanations* Cassiodorus continually refers to Jesus as "Christ the Lord,"[21] and statements in the final verses of the Apocalypse confirm "that Christ is the Lord himself."[22] On Rv 16.19, where a great city is split into three parts, Cassiodorus uses the trifurcation to comment that "the city of God, as I think, was founded on the faith of the Trinity." Perhaps in light of the presence in Italy of Ostrogoths, who held a non-Trinitarian theology and an Arian (*homoian*) Christology,[23] these comments served as an affirmation of Catholic teaching regarding the Trinity and the divinity of Jesus Christ. This comment may be an example of what Cassiodorus said in the prologue to the work, that a diligent reader will be able to learn in it what is orthodox.

Cassiodorus's comment on Rv 1.9 shows that he believed John was exiled by the emperor Domitian, which was the dominant view in early Christianity concerning the date of the Apocalypse,

19. Besides Tobit, other Jewish literature mentioning seven angels includes *1 Enoch* 20; *2 Enoch* 19.1; and *3 Enoch* 17.1 (*OTP*, 1:23–24, 133, 269). See Bogdan C. Bucer, "The Divine Face and the Angels of the Face," in Robert J. Daly, ed., *Apocalyptic Thought in Early Christianity* (Grand Rapids, MI: Baker, 2009), 143–59 at 150–52.

20. For the seven spirits as seven angels in the Greek exegetical tradition, see Oecumenius, *Commentary on the Apocalypse*, on Rv 1.4; 4.5 (FC 112: 24, 56), who wrote that this interpretation came from Clement of Alexandria's *Stromata* 6.16; and Andrew of Caesarea, *Commentary on the Apocalypse*, on Rv 1.4; 3.1; and 4.5–6 (FC 123: 57, 73, 83), who wrote that this interpretation came from Irenaeus of Lyons.

21. On Rv 1.5; 2.8; 3.1; 7.16; 12.13–14; 14.1; 19.7; 20.11.

22. On Rv 22.16.

23. The Homoians believed that Christ is *similar to* the Father, whereas Catholics of the Nicene faith believed that Christ is of the same substance (*homo-ousia*) as the Father.

but certainly not the only one.[24] Also in that chapter, Christ's robe symbolizes his priesthood; his golden girdle, the integrity of his actions; his white hair, his eternality; his feet, his preaching; and his voice, wisdom.

In the letters to the seven churches in Rv 2 and 3, Cassiodorus sees the *angel* of each church as its "bishop."[25] The candlestick, which the Lord threatens to remove from the bishop of Ephesus, indicates his good works;[26] and the morning star promised in Rv 2.26–28 to those who overcome is a glorious resurrection. Walking in white garments speaks of living with clean consciences.[27]

On Rv 4.1–2, where a voice said to John: *Come up here*, Cassiodorus views John's ascension to heaven as mental. The twenty-four elders of Rv 4.4 indicate for him "a number of fullness"; the four living creatures of Rv 4.6 represent the four evangelists; and the six wings in Rv 4.8 show the age allotted to the world before its consummation. The book in Rv 5.1 has writing on the inside and outside "because in the law some things are still obscure and some things are known to be clear." The odors in Rv 5.8 represent the quality of good deeds, and the harps "signify the perfect harmony of faith and works." Concerning the horsemen of the Apocalypse in Rv 6, the white color of the first horse represents a truly pure life, while the redness on the second indicates the shed blood of the Lord.

The one hundred forty-four thousand sealed ones of Rv 7.3–8 and 14.1–5 are interpreted as "the complete number of all of the blessed" and seem to be the same people as the multitude in Rv 7.9–16. They are virgins in that they do not commit fornication spiritually.[28] The seal on the foreheads of those in Rv 9.4 is the sign of the cross. Cassiodorus's version of Rv 8.11 had *Absentium* as the name of the star; and the king of the abyss in Rv 9.11 is depicted as *Exterminator*. These

24. The variety of opinions in early Christianity concerning under whose reign the Apocalypse was written includes Tiberius, Claudius, Nero, Domitian, and Trajan. See my essays "The Date of the Book of Revelation" and "John's Exile by Nero" in Francis X. Gumerlock, *Revelation and the First Century* (Powder Springs, GA: American Vision, 2012), 21–51.

25. On Rv 2.1, 8, 18; 3.7.

26. On Rv 2.5.

27. On Rv 3.5.

28. On Rv 14.3–5.

names derive from an Old Latin version of the Apocalypse of the African type, which Cassiodorus is known to have employed.[29]

For Cassiodorus, chapter 11 of the Apocalypse is mainly about the three and a half years "at the end of the world" when the Antichrist will reign. At that time Enoch and Elijah will appear, will be martyred, and will ascend to heaven. Chapter 12, according to Cassiodorus, concerns Jesus Christ and his mother, as John was joining "past things with future things." These past things include Mary's preservation for three years in Egypt (cf. Mt 2.19–23) and Christ's ascension to heaven. The war between Michael and the dragon in Rv 12.8, he says, "happened at the beginning of the world." In chapter 13 John returns to the time of the end of the world. The visions of the beasts, according to Cassiodorus, refer to the deeds of the Antichrist in the last days. These include his making war against the saints, speaking blasphemies against God, performing miraculous signs, and creating an idol that will be "worshiped with great devotion." Rv 14.14–19 describes the Second Coming of Christ and his judgment of the wicked at the end of the world.

Cassiodorus gives two interpretations of Babylon in chapters 17 and 18. Some, he says, think that it refers to Rome because of its description of seven hills and its worldwide authority. But Cassiodorus prefers to understand it as signifying the empire of evildoers (on Rv 17.7). On Rv 19.17–21 those "flying through heaven" symbolize holy people. Similarly, the birds in that section signify holy people.

The thousand years of Rv 20 are a figure of synecdoche, a whole number that signifies a part. They are not the duration of a future earthly kingdom, but started at the nativity of the Lord, and their end remains unknown to humans (on Rv 20.2, 7). Satan is now bound, barred from deceiving people among the nations who are going to believe (on Rv 20.3, 7). The "first resurrection" is the resurrection in faith "by which we are renewed by water and the Holy Spirit" (on Rv 20.5). The general resurrection for the Last Judgment, when each person's deeds are justly recompensed, is described in Rv 20.11–15 and 22.12. The gems of the New Jerusalem represent the beauty and diversity of the saints (on Rv 21.11–20); and the "tree of life" is the cross of Christ (on Rv 22.14).

29. Gryson, *Commentaria minora*, CCSL 107: 106–7; Gryson, ed., *Vetus Latina*, 26/2, Apocalypsis Johannis (Freiburg: Herder, 2000–2003), 370–71, 390.

*Sources.* Concerning the sources behind Cassiodorus's *Brief Explanations on the Apocalypse*, his *Institutes*, written about twenty years earlier in 560, provide insight. In that work Cassiodorus mentioned six commentaries on the Apocalypse in his library at the Vivarium. He wrote:

> But the Apocalypse, which diligently leads the minds of readers to heavenly contemplation, and makes them discern in their mind what the angels are blessed to see, is seen in the explanation of Jerome.
>
> About this book also the bishop Victorinus, often mentioned [above], has written briefly on certain very difficult passages.
>
> Also Vigilius, an African bishop, wrote in a very full and diligent narration about the understanding of the thousand years, which are contained in the aforementioned Apocalypse, and from which a great question arises in some.
>
> Also Tyconius the Donatist on this volume has written some things which are not to be rejected, but some things he has mixed with the dregs of his poisonous dogma. While reading it, inasmuch as I was able to discover, I have marked competently (as I think) "Christian" near the good sayings and "unchristian" near the bad ones. This also we urge you to do similarly in [the writings] of suspect expositors, so that the mind of the reader is not perchance disturbed, confused by the mixture of nefarious teaching.
>
> About this volume Saint Augustine in his books *On the City of God* admirably and diligently has opened up many things.
>
> Also in our own times the aforementioned Apocalypse was explained with zeal, minutely and diligently, in five books of bishop Primasius, an African prelate.[30]

The six commentaries mentioned above include the original commentary of Victorinus, Jerome's recension of it, and Tyconius's *Exposition of the Apocalypse*.[31] Cassiodorus mentions that Augustine's

---

30. Cassiodorus, *Institutes* 1.9. PL 70: 1122. Translation mine.

31. Victorinus's *Commentary on the Apocalypse* and Jerome's recension of it are in Iohannes Haussleiter, ed., *Victorini episcopi Petavionensis opera*, CSEL 49 (Vienna: Tempsky, 1916). They were more recently edited in Roger Gryson, ed., *Victorinus Poetovionensis. Opera quae supersunt*, CCSL 5 (Turnhout: Brepols, 2017). An English translation of it is in William C. Weinrich, trans., *Latin Commentaries on Revelation* (Downers Grove, IL: Inter Varsity, 2011). Tyconius's *Exposition of the Apocalypse* was edited in Roger Gryson, ed., *Tyconii Afri. Expositio Apocalypseos*, CCSL 107A (Turnhout: Brepols, 2011). An English translation of it is in Tyconius, *Exposition of the Apocalypse*, trans. Francis X. Gumerlock, with introduction and notes by David C.

*City of God* uncovers the mysteries of the Apocalypse, undoubtedly referring to the end of that work, which explains passages in the Apocalypse related to the final persecution of Antichrist, the thousand years of Rv 20, the general resurrection, the Last Judgment, and the heavenly city. Cassiodorus's library also contained an otherwise unknown work, now lost, on the thousand years of Rv 20 from the late fifth century by Vigilius of Thapse (modern Ras Dimas near Mahdia, Tunisia).[32] Finally, Cassiodorus mentions the commentary of Primasius, an African bishop whom Cassiodorus had met during his residence in Constantinople.[33]

Since Cassiodorus's *Brief Explanations* was designed as a summary and introduction, it is not surprising that there are few, if any, quotations from other commentators in it.[34] But one can discern interpretations from earlier writers that Cassiodorus most likely remembered from his readings of those commentaries. Correspondences between his interpretations and earlier commentaries are indicated throughout the translation in footnotes. For example, his explanations of Christ's white hair in Rv 1.14 and the "morning star" in Rv 2.28 match those of Victorinus. His interpretation of "nations" in Rv 20.3, as those who are going to believe in Christ,

Robinson, FC 134 (Washington, DC: The Catholic University of America Press, 2017).

32. On Vigilius of Thapse, see Claudio Moreschini and Enrico Norelli, *Early Christian Greek and Latin Literature: A Literary History*, vol. 2 (Peabody, MA: Hendrickson, 2005), 426–27; D. Röwenkamp, "Vigilius of Thapsus" in Döpp and Geerlings, *Dictionary of Early Christian Literature*, 598; Henry Wace and William C. Piercy, eds., *A Dictionary of Christian Biography* (Peabody, MA: Hendrickson, 1994), 1017; Manlio Simonetti, "Letteratura antimonofisita d'Occidente," *Augustinianum* 18 (1978): 505–22. His genuine works that survived, collected in PL 62, include *Contra Eutychetem* and *Contra Arrianos, Sabellianos, Photinianos dialogus*, the latter of which was recently edited in P. M. Hombert, ed., *Vigilius Thapsensis. Contra Arrianos, Sabellianos, Photinianos dialogus*, CCSL 90B (Turnhout: Brepols, 2017).

33. The Apocalypse commentary of Primasius is in A. W. Adams, ed., *Primasius episcopus Hadrumetinus. Commentarius in Apocalypsin*, CCSL 92 (Turnhout: Brepols, 1985). On the personal association of Primasius and Cassiodorus in Constantinople, see *Introduction to Divine and Human Readings by Cassiodorus*, trans. with introduction and notes by Leslie Webber Jones (New York: Columbia University Press, 1946), 21.

34. The closest thing to direct quotations are short phrases of Cassiodorus on Rv 20 and 21, which have parallels in Tyconius and Primasius. In the translation these are indicated with quotation marks and appropriate references in footnotes.

corresponds with that of Jerome. Cassiodorus's futuristic view of
the Apocalypse matches the commentary of Victorinus more than
that of Tyconius, who believed that the Apocalypse was mainly
about the wars and struggles of the Church between the Incarnation and the Second Coming of Christ. Nevertheless, Cassiodorus
prefers Tyconius's interpretation of Babylon as the empire of evil
people rather than Victorinus's view that it represents the city of
Rome.

Tyconius is mentioned by name in the prologue and twice in the
commentary: on Rv 9.10 and 11.5. The influence of Tyconius's view
that the Church is bipartite, made up of good and evil people, may
be seen in Cassiodorus's comment on Rv 3.4, where Cassiodorus
mentions the part of the church at Sardis that followed the will of
the Lord. When Cassiodorus comments on Rv 12.1–4, saying that
John was "joining past things with future things," he is echoing a
hermeneutical principle of Tyconius. Cassiodorus, however, does
not mention the concept of "recapitulation," so often expressed in
Tyconius's *Exposition*, nor does Cassiodorus speak of a great eschatological separation of hypocrites from the true Church, another
prominent feature in Tyconius's exegesis of the Apocalypse.

Cassiodorus reiterates Primasius's view that the "angels" of the
churches in Rv 2 and 3 refer to their bishops. In this interpretation,
Cassiodorus departed from Tyconius, who thought that "angel" in
those passages was a metonymy for the Church itself.[35] Cassiodorus
also follows Primasius in his interpretation of the vision in Rv 17.17–
21, of the thousand years of Rv 20 as a figure of synecdoche, and of
the gems on the foundation stones of the New Jerusalem as representing the saints (on Rv 21.19). The influence of Augustine's explanation of the thousand years of Rv 20 in Book 20 of his *On the City
of God* is apparent in Cassiodorus's explanation of the same. These
include his opinion that the thousand years started at the Incarnation of Christ, that Satan is now bound, prohibited from deceiving
the Church, and that the first resurrection is the regeneration of the
soul by faith and in baptism.

Cassiodorus's comments on Rv 20 also most likely reflect the
contents of the aforementioned lost treatise on the thousand years

---

35. Tyconius, *Exposition of the Apocalypse*, on Rv 1.19–20, CCSL 107A: 111–13.

by Vigilius of Thapse. Some in the late fifth century were using the thousand years of Rv 20 to predict that the end-time events, such as the rise of Antichrist and Second Coming of Christ, would occur near the end of the fifth century. They did this by using passages in Daniel. Their view was that the seventy weeks of years (490 years) prophesied in Dn 9.25 had a double reference to both the Incarnation of Christ and his Second Coming.[36] These 980 years, they said, corresponded with the thousand years of Rv 20, explaining the last twenty years as a time of great sorrow, persecution, and evil. They buttressed this idea by showing the similarity between Michael the archangel in Dn 10.13, 21, and the binding of the devil by an angel in Rv 20.[37] Thus they expected the end-time events and expiration of the thousand years to occur between 490 and 510 AD. Vigilius's lost treatise on the millennium most likely argued against the view that the end of the thousand years could be predicted from Scriptures. Cassiodorus's comments about the end of the millennium being "altogether unknown" to humans (on Rv 20.2, 7) probably reflect the argument of Vigilius's lost treatise.

In at least two places in Cassiodorus's *Brief Explanations*, on Rv 1.15 and Rv 4.8, his comments are similar to those of Apringius's *Tractate on the Apocalypse*, written on the Iberian Peninsula in the mid-sixth century.[38] Also, on Rv 1.18 Cassiodorus disagrees with an opinion found in Apringius's treatise. Therefore, it is possible that Cassiodorus had read Apringius's work. Also, since Cassiodorus spent over a decade in Constantinople, it is very likely that during that time he was influenced by Eastern interpretations of the Apoc-

36. They interpreted the phrase in Dn 9.25 *ab exitu sermonis* or *ab exitu verbi* as both "from the issue of a decree" of a Persian king to the Incarnation of Christ, and "from the going forth of the Word" from Mary to his Second Coming. Jerome reported that this was the view of Apollinaris of Laodicea (*Commentary on Daniel*, on Dn 9.24–27; Archer, *Jerome's Commentary on Daniel*, 104); and Augustine (*Epistle* 199.19. FC 30: 370) reported this as the view of Hesychius of Dalmatia. See also Filastrius of Brixia, *Book of Diverse Heresies*, 107.1 (CCSL 9: 269–70), who rejected it.

37. On the correspondence of the seventy weeks prophecy and the thousand years of Rv 20, see Quodvultdeus of Carthage, *On the Promises and Predictions of God*, Dimidium Temporis 4.6, CCSL 60:193; and Apringius of Beja, *Tractate on the Apocalypse*, on Rv 20.9–10, in Weinrich, *Latin Commentaries on Revelation*, 51.

38. Apringius's *Tractate on the Apocalypse* was edited by Gryson in *Commentaria minora*, CCSL 107.

alypse, for example, the view of the "seven spirits" of Rv 1.4 as seven angels.

*Summary.* Cassiodorus's *Brief Explanations of the Apocalypse* seems to have circulated very little in the Middle Ages. Only one manuscript containing it has been found; it is mentioned in no medieval library catalogues; and none of the medieval commentators on the Apocalypse appear to have made use of it.[39] Nevertheless, it is useful in that one is able to see how the Apocalypse was interpreted at the end of the sixth century and what sources influenced Cassiodorus. For the most part, he saw the Apocalypse as a prophecy of future events that will occur near the end of the world. These include the rise and persecution of the Antichrist and the return of Jesus to execute the Last Judgment. Cassiodorus, however, was eclectic in his approach, incorporating what he considered the best interpretations from his readings of Victorinus, Tyconius, Jerome, Augustine, Primasius, Vigilius, and possibly Apringius.

39. On the lack of readership of Cassiodorus's *Complexiones* in the Middle Ages, see Poole, "The Western Apocalypse Commentary Tradition of the Early Middle Ages," 117–18.

# TRANSLATION

## CASSIODORUS, *BRIEF EXPLANATIONS ON THE APOCALYPSE*

### Prologue[1]

ERHAPS SUITABLY we have joined the Apocalypse of blessed John to these Acts,[2] because it describes the heavenly kingdom in a wonderful narration, and since such a dwelling place will be granted to men such as these.[3] We have arranged this [treatise] to be divided into thirty-three chapters, [corresponding to] the age of Christ the Lord, whereas also thirty signifies the highest height of the heavens, and [with this number] the Holy Trinity's perfection, which commands our adoration, is associated.

It is a difficult task to choose to touch briefly on obscure sayings, when we want to explain these things more extendedly, as they should be. But Tyconius the Donatist subtly and diligently explained this book. (God, by his providence, for our salvation, makes an antidote from poison.) Because of the necessity for us to be brief in design, some interpretations that are in accordance with a novel and perverse teaching are recognizably necessary to omit, as we seem more to introduce our reader [to the book] than to satiate him. But without injury to his intelligence he will find in it what an orthodox and careful reader seeks.[4]

1. This prologue to the *Brief Explanations on the Acts of the Apostles and Apocalypse of John* (*Complexiones Actuum Apostolorum et Apocalypsis Johannis, Prologus*) is in CCSL 98B: 122 and PL 70: 1381–1382. Above I have translated the material in the prologue about the Apocalypse, but not about Acts.

2. This section of Cassiodorus's *Complexiones* combines the Acts of the Apostles with the Apocalypse.

3. The blessed ones whose deeds were narrated in the Acts of the Apostles.

4. Thus the Apocalypse is not irrelevant, as some, who rejected the Apocalypse,

## Chapter One

1. [1] *The Apocalypse of Jesus Christ, which God gave to him to make known to his servants,* etc. A certain prologue[5] is put first so that the dignity of the present book may be indicated briefly. For the apostle John says that a vision about the end of the world was shown to him by Christ the Lord. Both through whom it was shown and why it was shown are recounted, so that, with such truth revealed, both the devoted person might gain confidence and the conscience of unbelievers might obtain fear. [3] Also, one who chooses to read and to keep these things is praised so that, having been invited by such promises, the soul of devoted people may be kindled more ardently.

2. [4] *John, to the seven churches which are in Asia, grace to you and peace,* etc. The apostle John says that he is writing to the seven churches which have been established in Asia. He greets them, and wishes them peace and for grace to come from Christ the Lord and from the seven angels[6] who, as is read, stand before the throne of the Lord, as in the book of Tobit where the angel Raphael said: "I am one of the seven angels who stand before the throne of the glory of God."[7] But who this Lord is, "who is, who was, and who is to come,"[8] he makes known through an obvious statement, [5] testify-

---

thought. See, for example, Epiphanius, *Panarion* 51.32.2 (Philip R. Amidon, trans., *The Panarion of St. Epiphanius, Bishop of Salamis: Selected Passages* [New York: Oxford University Press, 1990], 187), who recorded the thoughts of certain persons who questioned the relevance of the Apocalypse, saying, "What good does the Revelation of John do me when it tells me about seven angels and seven trumpets?" In early medieval Spain some clerics refused to read or preach from Revelation, prompting the Fourth Council of Toledo in 633 to threaten excommunication to any cleric who refused to preach from it. See Alberto del Campo Hernandez, *Comentario al Apocalipsis de Apringio de Beja* (Navarra, Spain: Editorial Verbo Divino, 1991), 49; and E. Ann Matter, "The Pseudo-Alcuin 'De Septem Sigillis': An Early Latin Apocalypse Exegesis," *Traditio* 36 (1980): 111–37 at 117, note 11.

5. Cassiodorus is referring to Rv 1.1–3 as the prologue to the Book of Revelation, not to his own prologue to his *Complexiones*.

6. Cf. Oecumenius, *Commentary on the Apocalypse*, on Rv 1.4; 4.5 (FC 112: 24, 56), who wrote that this interpretation came from Clement of Alexandria's *Stromata* 6.16; Andrew of Caesarea, *Commentary on the Apocalypse*, on Rv 3.1 and 4.5–6 (FC 123: 73, 83), who wrote that this interpretation came from Irenaeus of Lyons.

7. Tb 12.15.

8. Rv 1.8.

ing that he is Christ the Lord, who redeemed us with his precious blood.[9] [7] He also tells how he will come in his Second Advent and how he will be seen by people in his glorious power. [8] For he is "the first and the last"[10] and the Almighty, which he also established with that statement about his divinity.

3. [9] *I, John, your brother and partner in tribulation,* etc. The apostle, when he was on the island Patmos, having been sent happily into exile by the emperor Domitian on account of the word of the Lord and [10] having been warned on the Lord's day by a loud voice, [11] said that he heard [a command] that he should write down the things which he saw, and should send them to the seven churches whose names are read as written. [12] And having turned suddenly toward the voice of the Lord, he saw seven shining candlesticks, [13] and in the midst of them Christ the Lord, whose appearance he explains through mystical comparisons. For he was clothed in a robe which there is no doubt pertains to his priesthood.[11] He was "girt over the paps with a golden girdle" because of the fact that the integrity of his actions was shining. [14] Indeed, his head and hair, which were white, show that he is the most Ancient of Days.[12] Moreover, his "eyes were like a flame of fire" because he penetrates all things with his gaze, and "no one is able to hide himself from his heat."[13] [15] His feet were similar to brass because he is found to be very strong and very glorious in his preaching.[14] "His voice was as the sound of many waters," since rivers of wisdom proceed from it. [16] But concerning the seven stars, he explains below.[15] "And from his mouth came a two-edged sword" signifies the mysteries of the New and Old Testaments.[16] His face shone as the sun, since whatever it does not gaze upon is in a shadow.

[17] Terrified by this vision, he testifies that he "fell down be-

9. Cf. 1 Pt 1.18–19.

10. Rv 1.17; 2.8.

11. Cf. Primasius, *Commentary on the Apocalypse,* on Rv 1.13. CCSL 92: 17.

12. Cf. Dn 7.9, 13, 22; Victorinus, *Commentary on the Apocalypse,* on Rv 1.14. CSEL 49: 20.

13. Ps 18.7. Psalm numbering is according to the LXX.

14. Cf. Rom 10.15.

15. On Rv 1.20.

16. Cf. Victorinus, *Commentary on the Apocalypse,* on Rv 1.16. CSEL 49: 22; Primasius, *Commentary on the Apocalypse,* on Rv 1.16. CCSL 92: 20.

fore his feet." The Lord said to him, "Rise, fear not," establishing himself to be the first and the last, [18] and asserting that he "has the keys of death and hell." Moreover, remember that these and other visions of this kind, which the Lord deigned to declare to his servants, were formed for a particular time and to show the quality of the things [they represent],[17] the [true] nature of his divinity remaining in its lofty state.[18] That very nature of divinity, however, as it [truly] is, is proven still to have been shown to no living human.[19] This [nature], as it [truly] is, he promises to reveal to clean hearts after the resurrection.[20]

4. [19] *Therefore, write the things which you have seen, and which are, and which must happen after these things.* [20] Now on the seven candlesticks and the seven stars, Christ the Lord explains to him the mysteries that John had seen, saying that the shining lights are these seven churches. But although the multitude of these [churches] is innumerable, seven are mentioned, that is, for the purpose of indicating perfection.

## Chapter Two

[1] Then he warns in a letter to the angel of the Ephesians, that is, to the bishop who truly was able to be admonished through the writing. [2] Indeed, he says that he knew his labors and patience in

17. Lat. *ad tempus esse pro rerum qualitate formatas.* Or *pro rerum qualitate* may mean "for a particular type of narrative." Cassiodorus uses this phrase again in his comment on Rv 14.14, where the vision of the Son of Man is different in that narrative, representing the Second Coming.

18. Cassiodorus does not believe that John's visions are "intellectual" visions, which, according to Augustine (*De Genesi ad litteram* 15), are those in which the visionary sees things as they properly are in themselves. Cassiodorus is saying that John did not see the divinity in its true and lofty state. As he says in the sentences following, such vision will come to clean hearts only after the resurrection. See 1 Jn 3.2.

19. Cf. Ex 33.20; Jn 1.18; 6.46; 1 Tm 6.16; 1 Jn 4.12.

20. Cf. Mt 5.8. On this point Cassiodorus disagrees with a view found in Apringius (*Tractate on the Apocalypse*, on Rv 1.17. CCSL 107: 46), which mentions John as "having beheld the full power of the deity" (*introinspecta omni uirtute deitatis*). Rather, Cassiodorus takes a position more like that of Irenaeus of Lyons (*Against Heresies* 4, 20.11. ANF 1: 491) and Primasius (*Commentary on the Apocalypse*, on Rv 1.17. CCSL 92: 20–21), the latter of whom wrote that the disciples were allowed to see only a *specimen* of his glory.

not wanting to cast out the false preachers, [4] but scolds him for neglecting charity, [5] to which [charity] he advises that he return with a repentant disposition, lest his candlestick, which clearly indicates good works, be removed or, as it were, snuffed out. [6] He praises him because [he hates] the deeds of the Nicolaitans, that is, shameful fornications, just as the Lord will condemn them with disgust. [7] Moreover, a reward is promised to those who overcome detestable vices, that they may eat food from the tree of life, which stands in the paradise of the Lord, where everyone is restored spiritually, [everyone] who is gathered in the kingdom of the Lord in eternal beatitude.

5. [8] *And to the angel of the church of Smyrna, write: The first and the last says these things*, etc. He advises that he should write to the angel of Smyrna, that is, to the bishop;[21] for that passage in the Acts of the Apostles testifies that a bishop is called an angel, where Peter comes and knocks on the door of the apostles, and it is said, "It is not Peter, but his angel."[22] He says that Christ the Lord, who once was dead and ever lives, [9] knows the quality and amount that they have suffered from unbelieving Jews. [10] Accordingly, if he also will choose to endure to the end, after being tested he will receive the crown of life forever. [11] For the one who will have overcome the evils of the world will not experience the punishment of the second death.

[12] Also he speaks to the bishop of Pergamum, indicating similarly: [13] "I know that you have kept the rule of patience among some depravities, that even when Antipas was enduring martyrdom you could not be deterred by any fear. But nevertheless I know that there are those in your midst who are joined to diabolical depravity. [16] And therefore return more quickly to the medicine of repentance, lest coming in judgment of those who are obstinate, I should avenge their evil with eternal punishment." [17] Moreover, to those overcoming the world, he promises manna and a white

21. Cf. Primasius, *Commentary on the Apocalypse*, on Rv 1.19–20. CCSL 92: 22.

22. Acts 9.15. Interestingly, Tyconius used this passage in Acts to prove that "angel" in Acts 9.15 meant Peter's own "spirit," and that John used the word "angel," not for the bishop of the church addressed in the letters in Rv 2 and 3, but as a metonymy for the Church itself. See Tyconius, *Exposition of the Apocalypse*, on Rv 1.19–20. CCSL 107A: 110. FC 134: 36.

stone, which indeed is found to be more precious than all pearls.

6. [18] *And to the angel of the church* which is in *Thyatira, write: The Son of God says these things,* etc. He says that it should be written to the angel, [that is,] to the bishop, as was already discussed, of the church of Thyatira, that the Lord, "who has eyes like a flame of fire and feet like fine brass," says these things, so that nothing is obscured for him [that is, the bishop] in his perception and so he does not grow weary in his preaching. [19] Indeed, he asserts that he knows the good things that he has done, along with his very commendable charity. [20] But in the midst of those things, [he asserts] that he is pained by evils, by a certain offense of his. For his congregation, which for the most part has fornicated with depraved behaviors, also has [a certain woman who] wants the name of prophetess, who ought rather to be called "Jezebel." [21] Unless she is converted, [22] very soon she will be cast onto a bed of sorrow; and grave judgment will come upon her fornication, [23] so that all the churches may know that the Lord renders to each person in accordance with the quality of their deeds. [24] Moreover, he advises the rest residing in that same church [25] to persevere in the accepted rules of the faith, [26] promising to victors that they would rule "the nations [27] with a rod of iron," [28] just as he also said had been granted to him by his Father. Also he promises that he will give to such people a glorious resurrection, which he signifies by mention of the star.[23]

## Chapter Three

7. [1] *And to the angel of the church* which is *in Sardis, write: He who has the seven spirits of God says these things,* etc. Christ the Lord, in whom resides the septiform Holy Spirit,[24] and in whose hand are seven stars, that is, universal power,[25] commands that it be said to the bishop of Sardis: "Indeed, in appearance you are alive, but in works you are dead. [2–3] And for this reason, with repentance intervening, strengthen yourself, that the things which have gone

23. Cf. Victorinus, *Commentary on the Apocalypse*, on Rv 2.28. CSEL 49: 38.

24. Cf. Is 11.2.

25. Cf. Tyconius, *Exposition of the Apocalypse*, on Rv 2.1. CCSL 107A: 113. FC 134: 40.

extinct in you may come alive through the medicine of satisfaction, so that you do not suffer the coming of fearful judgment as a thief, and that you may begin to sustain in your members the things that are important." [4] But since the people of the church live in different qualities of morals, he says that a part of Sardis is of the blessed, which part follows the commands of the Lord. And they will walk continually with the Lord [5] in white robes, that is, with very clean consciences. Henceforth they will not be erased from the book of life, and their names are mentioned in that laudable confession of his "before the Father and the angels."

8. [7] *To the angel* who is *at Philadelphia, the holy and true One says these things*, etc. The Lord, who is girt with the unique power of opening and closing, says that it should be written to the bishop of Philadelphia: "Since you are devoted to me in holy humility, [9] I am humbling before you the synagogue, that is, the congregation of Satan, so that [the synagogue], which formerly despised you by acting proudly, may come to the church to worship." Also he promises that [the church] will be protected from trials as the world gets worn out by various conflicts. [10] He also encourages him in his patience, [11] promising that he is coming quickly, and that another will not take his crown, [12] explaining what great things the Lord is going to give to his faithful ones.

[14] Also to the bishop of Laodicea he issues an indictment [15] that he ought to be either cold or hot, [16] lest if lukewarm he be spewed out of the mouth of the Lord. [17] For, since he puts confidence in his own strength, he is proven to be more wretched than all who are weak. [20] For he says that he is standing at the door, and he is knocking with repeated chastisement, so that when each one opens the door of his heart to him, he readily welcomes him to the supper of the Lord. [21] And [he says that] the one who is victorious may sit on the throne of his majesty, just as the Victor himself is distinguished as having sat down on the throne of his Father.

## Chapter Four

9. [1] *After these things I saw a door opened in heaven, and behold, a voice*, etc. After being called, John [2] ascended to heaven by contemplation of his mind and saw sitting on the throne the Lord, [3] whom he

associates through figures of speech with colors of gems. [4] There twenty-four elders, which indicate a number of fullness, "were sitting around the throne clothed in white." [5] Moreover, "from the Lord's throne proceeded flashes of lightning and voices and peals of thunder," before which were seven spirits, that is, angels of God. [6] But before the throne was seen "as it were, a sea of glass," through which the quality of this world is indicated:[26] a sea because it is subject to fluctuation; glass because it is recognized as fragile.

Before the throne and around the throne were stationed four living creatures [7] who are compared by a certain similitude to the four evangelists,[27] [8] having six wings on account of the age of this world, which is known to be able to be completed by such number.[28] By "full of eyes within" he signifies that the mysteries of their preaching are profound. [9] These [living creatures] were speaking praises to the Lord in perennial exaltation. [10] Indeed, the twenty-four elders, upon hearing the praise of the Lord, fell on their face "worshiping him who lives for ever and ever." And these also cast down their crowns in like manner.

## Chapter Five

10. [1] *And I saw a book in the right hand of* God *sitting upon the throne, written on the front and back*, etc.[29] Among these things he saw a book in the right hand of the Father sitting on the throne, written inside and out, because in the law some things are still obscure and some

26. Cf. Rv 17.5.

27. Cf. Victorinus, *Commentary on the Apocalypse*, on Rv 4.7–8. CSEL 49: 48; Tyconius, *Exposition of the Apocalypse*, on Rv 4.5–6. CCSL 107A: 70. FC 134: 65.

28. Here Cassiodorus is referring to an opinion common among early Christian writers, which said that the world has been allotted 6,000 years, one thousand for each day of creation. See, for example, *Epistle of Barnabas* 15 (ANF 1: 146); Irenaeus of Lyons, *Against Heresies* 5.28, 3 (ANF 1: 557); Hippolytus, *Commentary on Daniel*, Frag. 2.6 (ANF 5: 179). For a similar interpretation of the six wings in Rv 4.8, see Apringius, *Tractate on the Apocalypse*, on Rv 4.8. CCSL 107: 64; and Primasius, *Commentary on the Apocalypse*, on Rv 4.8. CCSL 92: 55.

29. While the Vulgate has *intus et foris*, meaning "inside and outside," the biblical version used by Cassiodorus had *intus et retro*. Hence the translation "front and back." In the comment below this verse, however, Cassiodorus has *intus forisque*, indicating his familiarity with another version of the biblical text. For Cassiodorus's text of the Apocalypse, see Introduction, p. 9, and n. 37 below.

things are known to be clear. It was sealed with seven seals; that is, it was perceived to have been sealed by the septiform Spirit,[30] since the mysteries of the Lord are always kept unknown up to their predetermined time. [2] Then, when the angel proclaimed [4] that "no one was found worthy" who could take and read it, John was afflicted with much weeping. [5] But one of the elders indicated to him that Christ the Lord was worthy "to open the book and to loosen its seals." [6] And having lifted up his eyes, he saw "a Lamb as if slain," having fullness of power and the purest preaching. [7] He took the book that was to be opened, as had been indicated. [8] To him "the four living creatures and twenty-four elders," with their harps and bowls full of various odors, that is, the quality of good deeds, [9] "were singing a new song, saying" that he, who was slain for the salvation of all, was worthy to be set apart with such honor. [10] To the faithful, he also conferred priesthood in a general manner and promised the kingdom of heaven. Moreover, the harps signify the perfect harmony of faith and works, but the bowls full of odors, as was said,[31] signify the prayers and supplications of the righteous.

11. [11] *And I looked and I heard, as it were, the voice of many angels around the throne,* etc. He also heard the voices of thousands of thousands of angels, speaking the praises of Christ the Lord: "He is worthy to receive glory, power, riches, and honor, namely, from the Father, because he suffered. To him every creature should give devoted homage." To them the four living creatures responded: "Let it be done!" at which the twenty-four elders, displaying agreement and falling on their faces, worshiped.

## Chapter Six

[1] Then, when the Lamb opened the first seal of the book that he had received, [2] a white horse was seen, which indicates a very pure life. And the one sitting upon it was holding an arrow, that he might conquer every adversity with his penetrating word.

[3] "When he had opened the second seal, [4] a red horse" was shown, which bore an image of the shed blood of the Lord. "And

30. Cf. Is 11.2.
31. Cf. Rv 5.8.

a great sword was given" to the one sitting upon it, that he might "take from the land the peace" of his subjects who were under great fear, and that he might cause his adversaries to destroy each other through mutual contention.

[5] When the third seal was opened, a black horse went out, showing, as we think, the power of domination over the impious, while the rider "held a pair of scales in his hand," since the impious are without doubt going to be judged. [6] To him the four living creatures said that the wheat and the barley reached the price of a penny, but the oil and wine are not to be harmed.

[7] "When the fourth seal was opened" …[32] [9] he saw under the altar of God the souls of martyrs [10] seeking swift vindication. [11] To them solace was given for their patience, having been promised that they would see it when the number of "their fellow servants was completed."

12. [12] *And I looked, when he had opened the sixth seal;* and behold, *a great earthquake occurred,* etc. Moreover, when the sixth seal was opened, he says through allegory that the earth trembled. "The sun became black," the moon was darkened with the color of blood, [13–17] and other things [are described], which were predicted to happen at the end of the world.

## Chapter Seven

[9] Then the multitude and congregation of the saints, that is, the one hundred forty-four [thousand],[33] in which number the complete sum of all the blessed is included, holding palm branches and "clothed in white robes," [11–12] resounded with the praises of angels.[34] [14] They have washed their robes in the blood of the Lord, and will rejoice in his sight in everlasting felicity; [16] neither will they, who are filled with the glory of Christ the Lord, any longer have need.

32. Cassiodorus's explanation of the fourth seal has been cut out of the manuscript probably through an error. See Gryson's edition (*Commentaria minora*, CCSL 107: 119): *explicationem quarti sigilli per homoeoteleuton excidisse manifestum est.*

33. Cf. Rv 7.4.

34. Like Tyconius (*Exposition of the Apocalypse*, on Rv 7.4–7, 9–10. CCSL 107A: 148–49. FC 134: 85–86), Cassiodorus views the 144,000 in Rv 7.3–8 as the same multitude described in the vision of Rv 7.9–16.

## Chapter Eight

13. [1] *And when he had opened the seventh seal, there was silence in heaven for half an hour.* Moreover, when the seventh seal was removed, [3] an angel came before the tribunal of God, carrying a golden censer in which he offers the supplications of the saints in the form of incense in the sight of Majesty.

[7] Then the first angel sounded a trumpet, and "hail and fire mixed with blood" were hurled upon the earth, the result being that they burned a third part of the earth.

[8] When the second angel sounded a trumpet, a burning mountain "was thrown into the sea," which, having become blood, [9] destroyed "a third part of the creatures and of the ships" that [the sea] was seen to contain.

[10–11] Indeed, when the third angel had sounded a trumpet, a great star, which is called "Absentium, fell from heaven upon a third part of the rivers and of the springs," which made the waters extremely bitter. Accordingly, those who drank [from them] died.

[12] When the fourth angel sounded a trumpet, it happened that "a third part of the sun, of the moon, and of the stars, was darkened"; and the day lost the same part[35] along with the night. [13] Then there was seen [someone flying] like an eagle, which said: "Woe, woe, woe to those who dwell on earth," [that is], those who will be woeful and will see such things of this magnitude.

## Chapter Nine

14. [1] *And the fifth angel sounded a trumpet, and I saw that a star had fallen from heaven*, and the rest. When the fifth angel sounded a trumpet, a star fell into a deep pit. [2] "And smoke went forth" from it, which darkened the air and the sun. [3] From it "locusts like scorpions came out." [4] They harmed neither grass nor tree, but only those who did not have the sign of the cross on their foreheads. [5] Tortured for five months as if stung by scorpions, [6] they groaned grievously in their pain. [10] Also, the appearance of the locusts is described in a mystery along with their power of harming,

---

35. That is, a third part.

which Tyconius explained briefly but thoroughly.[36] [11] Over them, he says, a terrible angel presides, whose name is "Exterminator."[37]

[13] When in like manner the sixth angel sounded a trumpet, [14] the four angels who were bound in the river Euphrates [15] were loosed. [17] These, causing terror with their horses and weapons, [18] were said to have killed a third part of humans, [21] who did not repent of their deeds.

## Chapter Ten

15. [1] *And I saw another strong angel coming down from heaven clothed with a cloud*, etc. He says that he saw another very strong angel clothed with a cloud, whose "face was as the sun." Moreover, "his feet were as pillars of fire." [2] And having "placed his right foot on the sea and his left on the land, [3] he shouted in a loud voice." [4] And [the seven peals of thunder] responded [to him with very secret words, which he] was warned [not to write down].[38] [5–6] Moreover, the angel swore that the world will no longer exist, [7] but when the seventh angel "will begin to sound his trumpet, it will be finished," which is entirely in agreement with his servants, the prophets of God. [8–9] Also, having been warned, [10] he "received from the angel a book" which, after eating it, was sweet in his mouth, but in his stomach it was rendered bitter: because the law of the Lord is sweet[39] when it is chewed, but bitter when it is consumed and then forgotten.

## Chapter Eleven

[1] Also, he took "a reed similar to a rod," with which he was ordered to measure the places which Christian people held. [2] But

36. Cf. Tyconius, *Exposition of the Apocalypse*, on Rv 9.7–10. CCSL 107A: 158–59. FC 134: 98–99. Tyconius said that the locusts represent false prophets.

37. Cassiodorus appears to have taken the Latin name *Absentium* for the star in Rv 8.11 and the name for this angel, *Exterminator*, from an Old Latin version of the Apocalypse of the African type. See Gryson, *Vetus Latina* 26/2, *Apocalypsis Johannis* (Freiburg: Herder, 2000–2003), 370–71, 390.

38. The manuscript has a lacuna. The words in brackets were conjectured by Gryson (*Commentaria minora*. CCSL 107: 120).

39. Cf. Ps 18.8, 11.

he [was ordered] to leave out [measuring] other places, which unbelievers were able to hold. These [unbelievers] are those who, at
the end of the world for the three and a half years when Antichrist
is reigning, will revel in the blood of the martyrs. [3] Also, there
was a mention of Enoch and Elijah, [8–9] that they will lie slain
publicly, unburied for three days, [11–12] until, called, they are seen
to ascend suddenly into heaven. Those enemies looking on were
stricken with great fear, [13] and they will offer glory to God with
great admiration.

16. [15] *And the seventh angel sounded a trumpet, and there were great
voices in heaven*, and the rest. When the angel sounded the seventh
trumpet, he relates that there were voices of those rejoicing in heav-
en, because at last the kingdom of God, which was seen by them,
arrived, and the things that were promised were fulfilled.

## Chapter Twelve

[1–4] But he touches upon a few things concerning the Lord Jesus Christ and his mother, and concerning the opposition of the
devil.[40] [5] Joining past things with future things, he says that God
ascended to heaven and [6] that his mother was to be preserved
at a certain time in secret places, that he might nourish her there
for three-and-a-half years.[41] This passage, as Tyconius relates, contains great mystery.[42]

17. [7] *And there was a war in heaven; Michael and his angels were bat-
tling with the dragon.* [8] He relates the war of the angel Michael with
the dragon, who fell headlong onto earth, so that he did not have
a place of blessedness any longer. Nevertheless, there is no doubt
that this happened at the beginning of the world. [11] Advancement
followed the deeds of the good when the devil fell, who now always
envies good, faithful people. But the lands and the sea are grave-
ly saddened when they experience malice of such great weight.

40. Cf. Tyconius, *Exposition of the Apocalypse*, on Rv 12.4. CCSL 107A: 176. FC
134: 123.
41. Cf. Mt 2.19–23.
42. Cf. Eph 5.32; Tyconius (*Exposition of the Apocalypse*, on Rv 12.6. CCSL 107A:
178. FC 134: 127) wrote that the woman nourished for one thousand two hundred
sixty days symbolizes the Church nourished on heavenly teaching from the birth
of Christ up to the end of the world.

[13–16] Again, there is a mention of Christ the Lord and his mother, in that the devil, believing that he could hurt the mother, sent from his mouth an immense river and thought that it would drown her. But she, having been taken to a very safe place, evaded the poison of diabolic fraud. [17] Nevertheless, that ancient author of evil did not desist from persecuting those who are known to be obedient to the Lord's orders.

### Chapter Thirteen

18. [1] *And I saw a beast rising up from the sea, having ten horns and seven heads.* In a type of the Antichrist, a great beast is described as rising from the sea. [2] This [beast], terrible in appearance, is formed with diverse members of ferocious animals. [4] It is said that this [beast] is going to make war [5] for three and a half years with the saints, with whose blood and by whose slaughter it is fed. [6] It is going to speak very blasphemous things against God. At the end [of the world] the faithless ones, who will not have the gifts of the Lord, will worship it. Nevertheless, this is described generally, [10] since he who wants to capture another will himself be captured; and he, with worthy compensation, will receive an exchange of the evils [he inflicted]. For here the saints suffer evils, but soon they arrive at their hope, as shown by the Lord.

19. [11] *And I saw another beast rising up, and it had two horns,* and the rest. Another beast is described as rising up from the earth in a type of the devil, that is, of the Antichrist, a truly savage beast, which is going to destroy many who are caught unaware. [13] At that time the Antichrist is going to perform many miraculous signs [14–15] in that he makes an idol, crafted skillfully with sacrilegious falsehood, to be worshiped with great devotion. [16] Also, the condition of the human race is described as so savage [17] that no one may sell to another or buy from another unless he is marked with the name of the beast, that is, with his devotion. [18] Then the appropriate number of the beast is explained under a certain mode of calculation.

### Chapter Fourteen

20. [1] *And I looked, and behold a Lamb standing on Mount Zion, and with him one hundred forty-four thousand,* etc. He says that he saw Christ

the Lord standing on Mount Zion, and with him one hundred forty-four thousand of the blessed who were bearing the names both of him and of his Father "written on their foreheads." [3–5] These have been polluted with no lie, no fornication concerning the faith. Nevertheless, this is best understood as consisting of all of the blessed.[43] These were singing a new song to the Lord, [new] because it was unable to be sung by anyone else. Then they are praised in a wonderful narrative.

[6] He says that he saw another angel who was evangelizing diverse peoples, [7] and that God ought to be feared by the nations, and that this was fitting for him because of the coming of his judgment.[44]

[8] A second angel, following [the first], said that Babylon, and likewise unbelievers, had fallen. This [city], filled with the wine of fornication, continued its drunkenness of error with its destructive behaviors.

[9] Also a third angel said: "If anyone worships the beast and his image, [10–11] he incurs a fall into the wrath of God." Moreover, there is a terrible and frightening description of their punishment.

21. [13] *And I heard a voice from heaven saying to me: Write: "Blessed are the dead who die in the Lord,"* and the rest. It was ordered by heaven that he should write down the things which were said, testifying: "Blessed are the dead whose labors have ended with their life." [14] He also saw a white cloud upon which the Son of Man was sitting, whose different likeness is suited to the nature of the narrative.[45] For he will come again in the [same] manner as he was seen

---

43. Tyconius likewise (*Exposition of the Apocalypse*, on Rv 14.2–4. CCSL 107A: 188. FC 134: 140) did not see the 144,000 as only males or only virgins in the flesh. Victorinus (CSEL 49: 82–83) believed the 144,000 were the number of those who will believe the two witnesses in the time of Antichrist. Cyprian, in *Ad Fortunatum* (ANF 5: 505), saw them as the assembly of Christian martyrs.

44. I have not included here the three additional words of conjecture in Gryson's edition, because the PL edition, which reflects the manuscript, reads well without the words of conjecture.

45. Lat. *pro rerum qualitate*. The vision of the Son of Man here differs from when he is seen by John in Rv 1.13–16. He is pictured here with a golden crown on his head, a sickle in his hand, and sitting on a cloud because, as Cassiodorus implies in the next sentence, this vision seeks to communicate his Second Coming for judgment. The same phrase *pro rerum qualitate* is used in Cassiodorus's comment on Rv 1.18.

by the apostles [going] into heaven.[46] Therefore, at that time he had "on his head a golden crown," the most glorious dignity of his majesty. In his hand he had a very sharp sickle, whose power the sinful generation at the end of the world should fear. [15] For, when the angel says: "It is time for reaping the harvest," which is acknowledged as being "now ready to be reaped," [16] he "thrust his sickle on the earth" and cut down wicked people with the greatest swiftness. [19] Again "an angel thrust his sickle on the earth" and swiftly cut off his clusters of grapes, which represent people swollen with malice. They were cast "into the winepress of the wrath of God," and their blood flowed "for a distance of one thousand six hundred stadia," which there is no doubt has mystical significance.[47]

### Chapter Fifteen

[1] He also relates that he saw seven angels, having in their power seven plagues, which are going to be inflicted by the indignation of the Lord. [2] Also, on a "glassy sea, mixed with fire, were standing" the martyrs, who completed the victory against the devil by the gift of the Lord. [3–4] And they were rendering a song to God with great exultation.

22. [5] *And after these things I looked, and behold the temple of the tabernacle of martyrs in heaven was opened.* After the temple was opened, where the martyrs were, [6] he says that he saw seven angels, carrying the plagues that were going to be inflicted on the people, that is, the unfaithful. And they were clothed in white robes, "girt with golden girdles around their chests."

### Chapter Sixteen

[15.7] [The angels] received the seven bowls in their hands [1] so that they might pour out upon the earth [4] and on the rivers diverse kinds of forces upon those who, having despised the voice of

---

46. Cf. Acts 1.11, that is, in the clouds.

47. Cf. Tyconius, *Exposition of the Apocalypse*, on Rv 14.19. CCSL 107A: 194. FC 134: 147; Primasius, *Commentary on the Apocalypse*, on Rv 14.19. CCSL 92: 220. Both Tyconius and Primasius wrote that the number sixteen (in sixteen hundred) is four squared, and that this quaternity represents the four regions of the world.

the Lord, were serving idols and perversities. [5–7] Then the glory of the Lord was sung by the mouth of the saints because appropriate compensation followed [the sins of the recipients of the bowls of wrath].

23. [8] *And the fourth angel poured out his bowl upon the sun,* and the things that follow. The fourth, [10] fifth, [12] sixth, and [17] seventh angels poured out the bowls that they had received, and the earth was stricken with such great force that a voice went out from the Lord saying, "It is done." [18] And immediately "voices and peals of thunder [sounded], and an earthquake occurred such as had never occurred from [the beginning of] the world." [19] Then he says that the city of God, as I think, was founded on the faith of the Trinity,[48] and that Babylon received what the divinity once prepared to send upon her, [20] and that all the powers and heights moved from their usual [places]. [21] When great hail fell and afflicted unbelievers, they began to blaspheme God, since this assault was so great that it could in no way be endured.

## Chapter Seventeen

24. [1] *And one of the seven angels having the seven bowls came,* and the rest. One of the angels who had the seven bowls of plagues promised John that he would show him that great Babylonian harlot, [2] who was famous throughout the whole world. [3] Then, transported in spirit, he "saw the woman sitting upon a beast," [4] adorned with linen and purple and gems. In her hand was a cup of blasphemy and crime, [5] but "on her forehead was written: Babylon, the mother of fornications and the filth" of the whole earth. [6] And she was also "drunk with the blood of the martyrs" cruelly [shed] and was very full of an abundance of crimes. At this he was amazed to see that everyone thought that she, who was fashioned with such deformity, was the mistress of the earth.

25. [7] *After these things I saw another angel* [*who said*]: *Why are you amazed? I will tell you,* and what follows. The angel interprets for John, who was amazed, who the harlot is whom he had seen sitting upon

---

48. Rv 16.19 continues: *the city was split into three parts.* Hence Cassiodorus relates the number three to the Trinity. Cf. Eucherius of Lyons, *Formulas.* CSEL 31: 59: *III ad trinitatem.*

the beast that had "seven heads and ten horns." [9] Some choose to interpret her as the Roman city that sits upon seven mountains and possesses the world with a singular authority.[49] Others speak better about Babylon, [saying] that its position, not [literal] mountains, is conveyed, and they describe lofty powers. [15–17] This [Babylon], he says, is to be destroyed by the peoples whom it seemed to have dominated earlier.[50] [12] Also, he relates that ten kings are going to hold authority on the earth, but one of them, who is called Antichrist, is to be reserved for the end of the world. [14] He indeed decides to prepare a war against Christ, but his iniquity[51] is defeated by the Lord, who conquers him.

## Chapter Eighteen

26. [1] *After [these things] I saw another angel descending from heaven, having great power.* He saw also another angel descending onto the earth, whose glory enlightened the whole world. [2] He said that the very powerful "Babylon has fallen, has fallen," [3] since she has not only committed acts of immorality with herself, but became an example of destruction to all nations. [4] Also another voice followed [saying] that the congregation of the faithful should swiftly go out from her, so that her ruin would not involve the people who believed in the Lord. [6] Moreover, he says that double should be paid back to Babylon, [7–8] who in a presumption of pride vaunted herself. [9] Then her kings [11] and merchants weep bitterly because she, who thought that she alone possessed the goods of the world, has perished in such a short time.

27. [15] *Also the merchants of these things, who were made rich, will stand far from her,* etc. [16–18] The words of those sorrowing and reckoning are still protracted on Babylon: that the one who was powerful in riches and mighty in authority was so suddenly brought to ruin. [19] Because of this "they throw dust upon their heads," mourn their beloved [city], and console themselves with excessive tears.

49. For example, Victorinus, *Commentary on the Apocalypse*, on Rv 17.6. CSEL 49: 132; CCSL 5: 249.

50. Concerning Babylon here, Gryson (CCSL 107: 109) understands Cassiodorus to mean "the empire of evil," and that Cassiodorus is referring to the opinion of Tyconius and Primasius.

51. Cf. 2 Thes 2.7.

[20] And having been converted, they say, "Rejoice over her, you saints," whom she willingly massacred in ungodly persecutions, which are very well known, because your blood has been avenged.

[21] After these things an "angel took a great millstone," and, having thrown it into the sea, said that "Babylon the great will be thrown down" with such great force [23–24] that it will no longer be fit for holding wedding feasts there, or for hearing, as it were, the sounds of sucklings, because it was filled with crimes and was an example of every conceivable vice.

## Chapter Nineteen

28. [1] *After these things I heard, as it were, the sound of great multitudes in heaven,* and the rest. After the things that were said of Babylon were fulfilled, [2–5] great praise came forth from the holy angels and from all the elders in heaven. [6] Thus those worshiping the Lord with resounding voices, like resounding peals of thunder, were singing "Alleluia" to the One who brought low the pride of the very evil harlot in deserved retribution. [7] They added a very delightful hymn [which said] that Christ the Lord was joined with his bride, that is, the holy Church.

[9] The angel said to John, "Write, for these are the words of God: Blessed are those who are called to the supper of the Lord." [10] He [that is, John], when he wanted to worship him, was prohibited, since the good angels do not want themselves, but God, to be worshiped. [11] Then, having lifted up his eyes, he saw sitting upon a white horse Christ the Lord, [12] who is described in a very wonderful and fearful manner, [13] having a "robe sprinkled with blood" because of the testimony of his passion. [15] A "sharp sword was proceeding from his mouth" because his word is proven to be powerful and very efficacious. [16] He also has this written on his thigh to signify his humanity: "King of kings, Lord of lords."

29. [17] *And I saw an angel standing on the sun, and he shouted in a loud voice, saying,* and the rest. By those flying through heaven, that is, holy men,[52] the angel was heard to say, "Come to the supper of the

---

52. Cf. Tyconius, *Exposition of the Apocalypse*, on Rv 19.17. CCSL 107A: 216, where he says that the birds represent "the churches." Primasius (*Commentary on the Apocalypse*, on Rv 19.17. CCSL 92: 269) calls them "spiritual people" (*spirituales*).

Lord." [18] It was obviously honorable for such men to be invited to his [the Lord's] feast. And so that the figure of the allegory given might be preserved, he speaks of diverse creatures, as it were, feasting on flesh, as on various people who are to be gathered into his Church. [19] The devil was also seen coming with a great army, about to make war against the members of Christ the Lord. [20] But captured, he was cast with his false prophet, the Antichrist, "into the lake of fire burning" mightily. [21] The rest of his associates, who followed the beast, are known to have been slaughtered by the sword of the Lord, and they became the allocated food for all the birds, that is, for the saints.[53]

## Chapter Twenty

[1] Then an angel descends from heaven [2] who, having taken hold of the dragon who is Satan, sent him into the abyss bound with a chain. And he "bound him for a thousand years," by which, through a figure of synecdoche, "a whole" is indicated "from a part."[54] When its end is, is held as altogether unknown. Nevertheless, by the consensus of the fathers they are computed from the nativity of the Lord.[55] [3] [Satan was bound] so that he might not, by having unchecked authority, deceive the nations who were going to believe.[56] But he says that at the end of the world, Satan will be loosed; and when Antichrist comes,[57] many martyrs and confessors

53. Cf. Tyconius, *Exposition of the Apocalypse*, on Rv 19.21. CCSL 107A: 217, where he says that "in every time the Church eats," meaning "spiritually consumes," "the bodies of its enemies." Primasius (*Commentary on the Apocalypse*, on Rv 19.21. CCSL 92: 270–71) comments that we should not think of the statement in a carnal manner, as if we believe that the saints are satiated on the flesh of the impious. Rather, when the saints see the damnation of the impious, they are said to be satiated by the knowledge of divine justice, which they do not comprehend perfectly now.

54. Primasius, *Commentary on the Apocalypse*, on Rv 20.4. CCSL 92: 276. Cf. Augustine, *On the City of God* 20.7; Marcus Dods, trans., *The City of God by Saint Augustine* (New York: Random House, 1950), 720.

55. Cf. Augustine, *On the City of God* 20.8; Dods, *City of God*, 722; Tyconius, *Exposition of the Apocalypse*, on Rv 20.2. CCSL 107A: 218. FC 134: 177.

56. Cf. Jerome, *Commentary on the Apocalypse*, on Rv 20.3. CSEL 49: 143; Augustine, *On the City of God* 20.8; Dods, *City of God*, 723.

57. Cf. Augustine, *On the City of God* 20.9; Dods, *City of God*, 725; Tyconius, *Exposition of the Apocalypse*, on Rv 20.3. CCSL 107A: 219. FC 134: 177.

will be brought forth. [4] Also, he saw the martyrs of God, who never received diabolic marks on their foreheads. [5] He says that the first resurrection is one in faith,[58] by which we are reborn by water and the Holy Spirit,[59] [6] in which "the second death has no" place. But the general [resurrection] of the faithful priests of Christ remains until the amount of the established time is completed.

30. [7] *And when the end of the thousand years will have come, Satan will be loosed from his prison*, etc. He says that after the thousand years Satan goes out of his prison where now he is recognized as being bound. But this passage also should be interpreted as "a whole from a part,"[60] since this [amount of time] remains unknown to humans. [Satan goes out] to deceive the nations that have been dispersed throughout the whole world. [8] When they [that is, Gog and Magog], with impious domination, invade "the camp of the saints," [9] divine fire soon extinguishes them. And he plunged "the devil who had seduced them into the lake of fire," where also it was told that the cruel beast [10] with his false prophet, the Antichrist, had been cast.

[11] He also saw a white throne, and sitting upon it Christ the Lord, [12–15] who in the future resurrection rewards the deeds of each with just compensation.

## Chapter Twenty-One

[1] Then, seeing "a new heaven and earth," [2] he also gazed upon Jerusalem adorned as a very elegant bride is accustomed to be "prepared for her husband." [3] And a voice was heard from heaven: "Behold, the tabernacle," which accordingly was promised, where it is given to men to dwell with God, [4] where all sadness caused by need disappears and it is known that eternal joy reigns.

31. [5–6] *And the One sitting on the throne said: Behold, I make all things new*, and the rest. He says that Christ the Lord told him that he

58. Cf. Jerome, *Commentary on the Apocalypse*, on Rv 20.1–3. CSEL 49: 141; Augustine, *On the City of God* 20.6; Dods, *City of God*, 718. See also Tyconius, *Exposition of the Apocalypse*, on Rv 20.5. CCSL 107A: 220. FC 134: 178; and Primasius, *Commentary on the Apocalypse*, on Rv 20.5. CCSL 92: 277–78.

59. Cf. Jn 3.5.

60. Tyconius, *Exposition of the Apocalypse*, on Rv 20.7. CCSL 107A: 220. FC 134: 179.

should write down the things that he saw and heard, because he is "the Alpha and the Omega," who makes new things and changes past things, and gives the water of life to those thirsting. [7] And whoever will have been faithful to him will possess his inheritance in the position of a son, [8] but unbelievers are to be cast into the burning lake filled with the stench of brimstone, which is very appropriately called the "second death."

[9] Moreover, one of the angels, who was reported to be holding the seven bowls of plagues, [10] led John onto a very high mountain. To him he showed Jerusalem coming down from heaven, [11] very beautiful with a variety of wonderful features, whose glories are compared to the most splendid of gemstones. [12–18] And the whole [city] is described in this manner, so that its beauteous diversity is portrayed to understand its great mystery.

32. [19] *The first foundation [stone], jasper; the second, sapphire; the third, chalcedony*, and the rest. The wondrous beauty of that Jerusalem is still being described, which also on each of its foundations is said to have very precious gems "of the saints."[61] [21] This [city], whose gates [equaled] the number of the twelve apostles, [25] was always open. Its street, covered with the purest gold, glitters; and all that adorns it surpasses every price in quantity. [23] It is known to shine not from the light of the sun, but from its own Maker. [27] There nothing defiled and nothing soiled is found.

## Chapter Twenty-Two

[1] Moreover, the "river of life proceeds from the throne of" the Lord. [2] In the middle of it, it slides away into transparent clearness. A forest of trees is said to adorn both banks of it, which trees "bear their fruit throughout each month." [5] There will be no night there, nor any need, since the Lord illumines and satisfies everyone. [7] Lastly, he [the angel] says that those who will have kept "the words of this book" with a faithful mind are blessed.

33. [8] *I, John, [am the one] who saw and heard these things. And when I had heard and had seen these things, I prostrated myself*, and the rest, up to the end. When John said that he had heard and had seen the words of this book, giving thanks, he wanted to worship the angel. [9] To

---

61. Primasius, *Commentary on the Apocalypse*, on Rv 21.20. CCSL 92: 296.

him [that is, John] it was answered by him [that is, the angel] that he should be regarded as one of the saints, not as the Lord, but that the One who made heaven and earth should be worshiped instead.

After these things he says [12] that the Lord is going to come quickly, who will judge the works of each one with discretion rendered. He says that [14] they are blessed who have cleansed their consciences[62] with good actions, so that they can have reliance on "the tree of life," that is, in the faith of the cross.[63] [15] For, outside, whoever have polluted themselves with defiled actions are to be excluded from the kingdom of the Lord.

[16] Through many diverse statements he confirms that he is Christ the Lord, [18–19] testifying that no one should either add or take away anything in this book. [20] He is revealed to be the One who has granted understanding of eternal life, warning[64] everyone to be ready, since he testifies with frequent repetition that he is going to come quickly. Amen.

---

62. Cf. Heb 9.14.

63. Cf. Tyconius, *Exposition of the Apocalypse*, on Rv 2.7. CCSL 107A: 114–15; Primasius, *Commentary on the Apocalypse*, on Rv 2.7. CCSL 92: 25.

64. Lat. *faciens*, "making."

# TESTIMONIES OF GREGORY THE GREAT ON THE APOCALYPSE

*Translated by*

MARK DELCOGLIANO

# INTRODUCTION

## *TESTIMONIES OF GREGORY THE GREAT*
## *ON THE APOCALYPSE*

*Author and Text.* St. Gregory the Great, who was Pope from 590 to 604, left behind a massive literary corpus. Perhaps best known is his *Moralia on Job*, which comments upon the biblical book of Job line by line according to the historical, allegorical, and especially moral senses.[1] In his *Book on Pastoral Care* Gregory reflects on the nature of the episcopal ministry and what would now be called spiritual direction.[2] He also left behind forty homilies on the Gospels and twenty-two on the allegorical meaning of Ezekiel 1.1–4.3 and 40.1–47.[3] His other literary remains include 854 letters, the *Dialogues on the Miracles of the Italian Fathers*, and a fragment of his

---

1. Marcus Adriaen, ed., *S. Gregorii Magni Moralia in Iob*, 3 vols., CCSL 143, 143A, and 143B (Turnhout: Brepols, 1979–1985); *Gregory the Great. Morals on the Book of Job*, 4 vols., Library of Fathers of the Holy Catholic Church 18, 21, 23, and 31 (Oxford: J. H. Parker, 1844–1850). A new six-volume translation by Brian Kerns has been published by Cistercian Publications: *Gregory the Great: Moral Reflections on the Book of Job*, Cistercian Studies Series 249, 257, 258, 259, 260, 261 (Collegeville, MN: Liturgical Press, 2014–2022).

2. Bruno Judic, Floribert Rommel, and Charles Morel, eds., *Grégoire le Grand. Règle pastorale*, 2 vols., SC 381 and 382 (Paris: Cerf, 1992); Henry Davis, trans., *St. Gregory the Great. Pastoral Care*, ACW 11 (New York and Mahwah, NJ: Newman Press, 1950); and George E. Demacopoulos, trans., *St. Gregory the Great. The Book of Pastoral Rule*, Popular Patristics Series 34 (Crestwood, NY: St. Vladimir's Seminary Press, 2007).

3. Raymond Étaix, ed., *Gregorius Magnus. Homiliae in Evangelia*, CCSL 141 (Turnhout: Brepols, 1999); David Hurst, trans., *Gregory the Great. Forty Gospel Homilies*, Cistercian Studies Series 123 (Kalamazoo: Cistercian, 1990); Marcus Adriaen, ed., *Sancti Gregorii Magni Homiliae in Hiezechihelem prophetam*, CCSL 142 (Turnhout: Brepols, 1971); Theodosia Grey, trans., *The Homilies of Saint Gregory the Great on the Book of the Prophet Ezekiel* (Etna, CA: Center for Traditionalist Orthodox Studies, 1990).

*Exposition on the Song of Songs.*[4] Though Gregory was an enormously popular author after his death and even during his lifetime, the sheer size of his extant corpus was daunting. Accordingly, collections of excerpts were frequently made—most frequently from the *Moralia*, the *Book on Pastoral Care*, and his homilies—in order to provide clerical and monastic readers, who did not have the time or the willpower to read the entire corpus, with a way of accessing the thought of Gregory in a more systematic and less time-consuming manner. This was a fairly common scholarly practice from antiquity through the Middle Ages.

The first person to produce a collection of excerpts from the writings of Gregory was Paterius, Gregory's notary, whose compilations date from the Pope's own lifetime.[5] In his *Book of Testimonies*, for each book of Scripture, Paterius gathered together all the interpretations of verses from that book that he could find, and arranged them according to their biblical sequence. Thus he intended to produce from the writings of Gregory something like a kind of running commentary on Scripture. Originally consisting of three parts (two for the Old Testament and one for the New Testament), all that survives from the *Book of Testimonies* is the first part, from Genesis to the Song of Songs.[6] Paterius's excerpts on the Book of the Apocalypse were in the third part, which is unfortunately now lost. It may have existed as late as 767 CE, around the time when

---

4. Dag Norberg, ed., *S. Gregorii Magni Registrum epistularum*, 2 vols., CCSL 140 and 140A (Turnhout: Brepols, 1982); John R. C. Martyn, trans., *The Letters of Gregory the Great*, 3 vols., Medieval Sources in Translation 40 (Toronto: Pontifical Institute of Mediaeval Studies, 2004); Adalbert de Vogüé and Paul Antin, eds., *Grégoire le Grand. Dialogues*, 3 vols., SC 251, 260, and 265 (Paris: Cerf, 1978–1980); Odo Zimmerman, trans., *St. Gregory the Great: Dialogues*, FC 39 (New York: Fathers of the Church, 1959); Patrick Verbraken, ed., *Sancti Gregorii Magni Expositiones in Canticum Canticorum, in Librum Primum Regum*, CCSL 144 (Turnhout: Brepols, 1963), 387–444; Rodrigue Bélanger, ed., *Grégoire le Grand. Commentaire sur le Cantique des Cantiques*, SC 314 (Paris: Cerf, 1984); Mark DelCogliano, trans., *Gregory the Great on the Song of Songs*, Cistercian Studies Series 244 (Collegeville, MN: Liturgical Press, 2012), 109–44.

5. On Paterius, see DelCogliano, *Gregory the Great*, 50–52.

6. André Wilmart, "Le recueil grégorien de Paterius et les fragments wisigothiques de Paris," *Revue Bénédictine* 39 (1927): 81–104. Wilmart's judgment was confirmed by Raymond Étaix in his "Le *Liber testimoniorum* de Paterius," *Revue des Sciences Religieuses* 32 (1958): 66–78. The authentic text is printed at PL 79: 683–916.

Ambrose Autpert wrote his commentary on the Apocalypse, in the preface of which he noted that "there are also extant some expository chapters on the Book of the Apocalypse by the holy man Pope Gregory of Rome that are drawn from his various works: though they are few in number, they are nonetheless most illuminating."[7] This seems to be a reference to the collection of Gregorian excerpts on the Apocalypse compiled by Paterius, though we cannot be certain since others besides Paterius produced compilations from Gregory's works. In any event, it seems that by the twelfth century two-thirds of the work of Paterius was lost for good, since at this time an anonymous compiler sought to reproduce the two lost parts of the *Book of Testimonies*, including the excerpts on the Apocalypse.[8] And so, the collection of fifty-five excerpts of Gregory on the Apocalypse translated in this volume, while attributed to Paterius, is the fruit of the toil of an anonymous twelfth-century scholar.[9] Drawn mostly from the *Moralia*, but also from the *Book on Pastoral Care* and the homilies, this pseudo-Paterian florilegium offers a representative selection of Gregory's comments on the Apocalypse.[10]

*Interpretation of the Apocalypse.* In his interpretation of Scripture Gregory takes what one might call a "grammatical approach." In other words, he relies heavily upon the techniques of reading incul-

7. CCCM 27: 5.

8. The inauthentic parts are printed at PL 79: 917–1136. The preface to the three parts (PL 79: 681–684) is not Paterius's either, but rather that of someone named Bruno.

9. PL 79: 1107–1122. There is another collection of Gregorian excerpts on the Apocalypse at PL 79: 1397–1424 attributed to a certain Alulfus. While this translation is based on the PL text, I have compared the Latin of each excerpt to the Latin of the best critical editions available today. In some cases, there are discrepancies between the PL and the critical edition. Most of these are mistakes, and I have tacitly used the Latin of the critical edition instead of the PL Latin text. But in some cases it is clear that the excerpter has purposely modified Gregory's text, and I note these cases in the footnotes.

10. According to the indices of the modern editions of Gregory's *Moralia*, *Book on Pastoral Care*, and homilies, the Pope cited or alluded to the Apocalypse 132 times (104 times in *Mor.*, 7 times in *Reg. past.*, 8 times in *Hom. Ev.*, and 13 times in *Hom. Ez.*). Including less than half of all possible texts, the anonymous compilation was by no means exhaustive.

cated in the Greco-Roman educational system.[11] Like many other patristic exegetes, Gregory used grammatical reading techniques to determine the literal or plain sense of Scripture, which was then the point of departure for all other interpretations, including the allegorical or figurative. In his interpretation of the Apocalypse, Gregory's comments on the plain sense of the scriptural passages are most often in contexts where he expounds upon the eschatology of the Apocalypse. In contrast, Gregory usually employs a figurative exegesis when he draws from verses of the Apocalypse insights on the spiritual life and the nature of the Church. This is not to say that Gregory's interest in the plain sense is limited to eschatological matters and his interest in the figurative sense to spiritual and ecclesiological matters. Rather, these are merely his general tendencies.

A few examples of his grammatical exegesis will be helpful. In his interpretation of Rv 14.4, he focuses on the plain sense of the verse to gain some eschatological insight (#32). Unsurprisingly, he connects the virgins who follow the Lamb wherever he goes with the one hundred forty-four thousand mentioned in Rv 14.3 who sing the new song before the throne of the Lamb, the four living creatures, and the elders. But then he offers two further reflections. First, what is this song they are singing? It is a song of rejoicing over the incorruptibility of their flesh. Second, what about the rest of the elect not included among the one hundred forty-four thousand virgins? True, says Gregory, they cannot sing this song, but they do hear it. Why? Because they have the fullness of charity, which leads them to rejoice in the sublime state of the one hundred forty-four thousand virgins, even if they do not share it. There is no figurative exegesis here. Gregory takes the verse at face value, connects it with the previous verse, and attempts to answer some questions that the verse raises for him, in order to understand more fully the eschatological life of the saints in heaven. Everything that Gregory does here comes from the toolbox of Greco-Roman grammatical reading techniques.

11. In his *L'esegesi di Gregorio Magno al cantico dei cantici* (Turin: Società Editrice Internationale, 1967), Vincenzo Recchia has stressed the grammatical and rhetorical methodologies that inform Gregory's exegesis of the Song of Songs. For an introduction to Gregory's grammatical approach in terms of both theory and practice, see DelCogliano, *Gregory the Great*, 65–84.

Gregory's figurative exegesis is also rooted in grammatical practices. One of the principal ways of understanding the meaning
of a text in grammatical analysis was discerning the reference of
words and sentences. Determining the reference meant answering
questions such as: What are the extra-textual realities to which the
words of the text refer? What are the extra-textual realities about
which the sentence is talking? Cross-referencing was a key grammatical method for establishing the reference of words.[12] In some
cases, the use of cross-references corroborated a claim about a
reference by showing that the same was said elsewhere. In other
cases, a cross-reference could be used to clarify or even establish
a reference. Discerning the reference, often by the use of cross-
referencing, plays a crucial role in Gregory's exegesis, especially in
his figurative exegesis. For him, in those verses of the Apocalypse
interpreted figuratively, certain words are symbols that point to realities of the spiritual life or the Church. Gregory takes great pains
to clarify that to which figuratively interpreted words and passages refer, usually by citing other passages of Scripture as cross-
references. An example of this is his interpretation of Rv 8.1, which
states that there was silence in heaven for half an hour (#19; cf.
#18). Here Gregory takes the word "heaven" as a figurative ref-
erence to "the soul of a righteous person," a reference he supports
by cross-reference to Is 66.1 and Ps 18.1. With the reference thus
established, Rv 8.1 becomes in Gregory's hands a verse about the
contemplative stillness that the righteous person experiences once
external distractions are eliminated. Rv 8.1 reports that this contemplative silence lasts about half an hour because contemplative
repose remains imperfect in this life and fleeting. A good portion
of the Gregorian excerpts on the Apocalypse employs similar
methods of exegesis to expound about spiritual and ecclesiological
topics, but also eschatological ones too. Note that for Gregory one
figurative interpretation of a word never excludes other possible
figurative meanings. "Heaven" can also figuratively represent the
"Church of the elect" (#18) or just the "Church" (#26). Similarly,
various references are discerned for "sun" (#24) and "gold" (#10,

12. On reference and cross-reference, see Frances Young, *Biblical Exegesis and
the Formation of Christian Culture* (Cambridge: Cambridge University Press, 1997),
119–39.

#34, #51). This is not to say that Gregory is in the habit of assigning any reference he wants to any word; rather, it is a question of knowing the customary speech patterns of Scripture and determining from these resources which scripturally sanctioned figurative reference for the word is applicable in a particular verse.

*Reconciliation of Apparent Contradictions.* Another feature of Gregory's grammatical exegesis is his interest in attempting to reconcile two passages of Scripture that appear to be contradictory. There are four examples of this in the excerpts on the Apocalypse. First, Rv 3.21 states that the one who conquers will sit with Christ on his throne, whereas in the Gospel Jesus says that his disciples will sit on twelve thrones (Lk 22.30; Mt 19.28). Even though the twelve thrones indicate universal judgment, and the single throne Christ's own unique power of judging, these two passages really refer to the same thing because the universal judgment, which the disciples receive, is but a delegation of Christ's own unique power of judging (#12). The second example deals with two discrepancies from the Apocalypse itself. In Rv 10.4 the angel commands John to seal the book, whereas in Rv 22.10 not to seal. Why is this? Because whatever was hidden at the beginning of the Church is revealed at its end (#21). Third, when interpreting Rv 19.10 Gregory notes that the angel forbids John to worship him, but in two Old Testament passages it was permissible to worship angels (Gn 19.1; Jos 5.13–15). The reason for this is that before the Incarnation angels looked down upon human nature as lower than themselves and allowed themselves to be worshiped by these inferior creatures. But after the Word's assumption of human nature angels realize that human nature has now been raised above themselves, and they dare not let humans worship themselves (#40). Finally, Gregory attempts to reconcile several New Testament passages that speak of heaven and earth passing away (1 Cor 7.31; Mt 24.35; Mk 13.31; Lk 21.33) with Rv 21.1, which says that there will be a new heaven and earth. So how is it that heaven and earth both pass away and remain? Gregory solves the puzzle by teaching that the present form of heaven and earth will pass away, but they retain their eternal nature as they are renewed (#48).

Even though the majority of the Gregorian excerpts on the Apocalypse are devoted to investigations of the spiritual life, given the breadth of the topic it is impossible to summarize them succinctly. Yet there are some notable passages. In one where Gregory is commenting on Rv 3.15–16, he explains that being in the spiritual state of lukewarmness is harmful because it means either that the one in the spiritual state of coldness (the sinner) has fallen short of leaving behind sin by not arriving at the spiritual state of hotness, or that the one in the spiritual state of hotness has lost fervor (#8). Elsewhere, Gregory describes in his interpretation of Rv 6.9–10 how the words of souls are their desires and remarks that the souls of the saints desire what God already wills for them (#14). Finally, in his exegesis of Rv 20.12 Gregory teaches that true self-understanding can be attained only by reflecting upon exemplars of good conduct; otherwise, we remain blind in the darkness of our true nature without looking at the light (#47).

*Ecclesiology and Eschatology.* Those excerpts which deal with ecclesiology and eschatology are fewer, and since they deal with more focused topics, some summary of Gregory's teachings can be offered. For Gregory, all individual churches make up the single universal Church (#1, #2, #44). The Church is a spiritual edifice built with the pillars of those who are steadfast in the work of God (#7). The preachers of the Church proclaim the glory of the heavenly kingdom (#3). The Church contains within itself the seven gifts of the Holy Spirit (#1, #2), is protected by the splendor of heavenly light, and despises all temporal things (#29). Yet the Church is also a mixed body of saints and sinners, of sinners who now seem to be elect but who in the final judgment will be unmasked as reprobate (#26, #35).

Central to Gregory's eschatology is the idea that at the end of the era of the Church, Satan is released from his bondage with all his strength for a final testing of humanity (#30, #43, #44, #45). Here Gregory bases himself on Rv 20.1–3. He is no millennialist, interpreting the "thousand years" not literally but as the present, long, indeterminate length of the Church's reign, however long it may be (#44, #45). In this period of his release in the last days the preachers of Satan rise up, displaying a pretense of holiness, as Antichrist makes his final attempts at seduction (#20, #25, #26, #29).

Gregory appears to identify Antichrist with Satan, whom he also calls the apostate angel (#43), the ancient enemy (#17, #27, #30, #45), the adversary (#28), the serpent (#43, #44, #45), and even Leviathan (#35, #43), though in one passage he seems to believe Antichrist is a "damned man" at the end of the world (#30). One of the chief goals of Antichrist and his preachers is to reveal certain members of the Church who appeared to be elect for what they really are, reprobates (#26, #35). Yet at the same time Enoch and Elijah will return and join in with the Church's preachers to help people resist these final temptations of Satan (#23). Nonetheless, the time allotted to Satan for this final testing is short, as he will soon be defeated by the archangel Michael and receive his final punishment (#27, #30). Those who conquer the ancient enemy in this final battle are victors (#17). The holy men who ruled themselves in this life are delegated by Christ to become judges in the final judgment (#12, #33). The saints in heaven come to possess full knowledge of God (#5). The Church receives double in the end: blessedness of soul (which is possible in this life) and incorruptibility of flesh (which is not) (#15). The saints in heaven are bound together by charity, and their hearts are perfectly transparent to each other (#32, #34, #51). They feast at the banquet of the Lamb in heavenly contemplation (#39).

*Sin, Grace, and Christology.* A few more excerpts deserve comment. In his interpretation of Rv 4.10 Gregory displays a very Augustinian notion of original sin and grace (#13). Since the fall of Adam human nature is disordered and corruptible, and any evil deed is a result of humanity's flawed condition, but through grace human beings can be changed to better inclinations and do good. Gregory is quite precise here, using typical Augustinian distinctions: grace gives first the will to do the good which was not willed and then the ability to do this good which is now willed. Gregory's indebtedness to theological standards is also seen in his endorsement of Chalcedonian Christology in his interpretation of Rv 19.16. Even though Gregory calls the body that Christ assumed from the Virgin a "robe," he is quick to point out that Christ's body is not one thing and he himself another thing. In other words, Gregory is careful not to fall into a kind of Christological dualism that would

separate too far Christ's humanity (his human body) from his divinity (his identity as the Word). In line with Chalcedonian Christology, Gregory affirms the unity of Christ as the single subject of
the Incarnation, suffering, death, and Resurrection (#42). A few
other excerpts deal with Christological issues in passing. Christ's
Resurrection and victory over death by his own power shows that
his power is equal to the Father's (#12, #42). Finally, Christ can be
called the "morning star" in two senses: first, by his Incarnation he
put sin to flight and proclaimed the eternal morning; and second,
by his Resurrection he overcame the darkness of our mortality and
showed us that the same was possible for ourselves (#52).

Since all these interpretations of the Apocalypse by Gregory
were made in passing as he commented on other passages of Scripture, they exhibit a variety and breadth that probably would not be
on display if Gregory had been specifically writing a commentary
on the Apocalypse. It is likely that Gregory knew of earlier Latin
commentaries like those of Victorinus or Tyconius, and perhaps
even some Greek commentaries from the time he spent in Constantinople (it remains debated whether Gregory had sufficient facility
in Greek to read eastern authors). While he adopted some of these
previous interpretations, he did not feel himself bound to them because he was not writing a commentary on the Apocalypse and as
a result had the freedom in his own interpretations to be distinct
and original. And so, Gregory stands out as a unique voice in the
history of the interpretation of the Apocalypse.

# TRANSLATION

## TESTIMONIES OF GREGORY THE GREAT
## ON THE APOCALYPSE

**N REVELATION** 1.4: *John to the seven churches that are in Asia.*
1. By the name of Arcturus, which, placed at the polar region of heaven, shines with the rays of seven stars, the universal Church is expressed. In the Apocalypse of John the universal Church is figuratively represented by the seven churches and the seven lampstands.[1] Containing within herself the gifts of sevenfold grace of the Spirit,[2] she glows with the brightness of highest virtue, shining as it were from the polar region of truth.

> From *Moralia* 9.11 [13], 29–34.
> CCSL 143: 465.

2. By the number seven is designated the universal character of the holy Church. Thus John in the Apocalypse writes to seven churches,[3] but what did he want us to understand by them, other than the universal Church? Indeed, to signal that the universal Church is full of the Spirit of sevenfold grace,[4] Elisha is described as having breathed seven times upon the dead boy.[5] Certainly, coming upon a lifeless people, the Lord as it were breathed seven

---

1. Cf. Rv 1.4; 1.20.
2. Also known as the seven gifts of the Holy Spirit. Based on Is 11.1-3, numerous Latin fathers identified these gifts as wisdom, understanding, counsel, fortitude, knowledge, piety, and fear of the Lord.
3. Cf. Rv 1.4.
4. See note 2 above.
5. Cf. 2 Kgs 4.32-37.

times upon it, seeing that in his mercy he bestows upon it the gifts of the Holy Spirit of sevenfold grace.[6]

> From *Moralia* 35.8 [18], 162–169.
> CCSL 143B: 1785.

On Revelation 1.20: *As for the mystery of the seven stars which you saw in my right hand, and the seven golden lampstands, the seven stars are the angels of the seven churches, and the seven lampstands are the seven churches.*

3. Since sacred Scripture is frequently accustomed to designating the Church's preachers by the name of "angels" because they proclaim the glory of the heavenly kingdom, we too can take "angels"[7] to mean "holy preachers." It is for this reason that John, when he writes in the Apocalypse to seven churches, speaks to the angels of the churches, that is, to those who preach to the people.[8] Hence it is said through the prophet: "And the angels of peace shall weep bitterly."[9] And likewise again, the prophet Malachi says: "The lips of a priest guard knowledge, and [people] look for the law from his mouth: for he is the angel of the Lord of hosts."[10] Hence Paul [too] says: "Great is the mystery of piety, which was manifested in the flesh, vindicated in the Spirit, seen by angels, preached to the nations, believed on in this world, taken up in glory."[11] Therefore, he who, after saying that the mystery of the divine dispensation[12] was "seen by angels," added that it was "preached to the nations," certainly by the name of "angels" designated holy preachers, that is, messengers of truth.

> From *Moralia* 34.7 [14], 38–53.
> CCSL 143B: 1742–43.

6. See note 2 above.

7. Here the excerpter omits two words, *hoc loco*, "in this passage," which in their original context referred to Jb 41.16.

8. Cf. Rv 1.20.

9. Is 33.7.

10. Mal 2.7.

11. 1 Tm 3.16.

12. Lat. *dispensationis mysterium*. The Latin term *dispensatio* is equivalent to the Greek term *oikonomia*, the "divine economy." Both refer to the fact of the incarnation and the entirety of Christ's incarnate existence, including his preaching, passion, resurrection, and ascension.

On Revelation 2.14: *You have some there who hold the teaching of Balaam, who taught Balak to put a stumbling block before the sons of Israel, so that they would eat and fornicate.*

4. Cain did not know the time of Antichrist and yet became a member of Antichrist as that evil deed deserved.[13] Judas was ignorant of the fierceness of Antichrist's tempting and yet succumbed to the might of his cruelty when tempted by greed.[14] Simon [Magus] was far removed from the times of Antichrist and yet associated himself with his pride by perversely seeking the power to do miracles.[15] And so it is that a wicked body is joined to its head; so it is that members are joined to members, when they do not know each other by acquaintance and yet are united to each other by their actions. For Pergamum had no knowledge of the books or the words of Balaam, and yet, because they followed his wickedness, they heard in a voice of rebuke from above: *You have some there who hold the teaching of Balaam, who taught Balak to put a stumbling block before the sons of Israel, so that they would eat*[16] *and fornicate* (Rv 2.14). And both times and places separated the church of Thyatira from personal knowledge of Jezebel, but because that [church] was similarly charged with crimes of behavior, Jezebel is said to dwell therein and to persist in [doing] perverse deeds, as the angel attests, who says: *I have something against you, that you allow the woman Jezebel, who calls herself a prophetess, to teach and to beguile my servants into fornicating and eating food sacrificed to idols* (Rv 2.20). Behold, because there could be found some who followed the conduct of Jezebel by reprobate actions, Jezebel is said to have been found there. For clearly an agreement of habits makes a depraved body one, even if places or times divide it. And so it happens that every wicked person who has already perished survives in his perverse imitators, and the worker of wickedness who has not yet arrived is already visible in those who do his works.

From *Moralia* 29.7 [15], 29–51.
CCSL 143B: 1443–44.

---

13. Cf. Gn 4.8.
14. Cf. Mt 26.15; Mk 14.11; Jn 12.6.
15. Cf. Acts 8.19-20.
16. That is, eat food sacrificed to idols.

On Revelation 2.17: *I will give him a white stone and a new name written on the stone, which no one knows except him who receives it.*

5. Indeed, to see perfectly the wisdom co-eternal with God is to possess it. Hence it is said to John about the reward given to the one who conquers: *I will give him a white stone and a new name written on the stone, which no one knows except him who receives it* (Rv 2.17). For in this life we are able to know or see something even without having received it. But when a new name is written on a stone, that is, in a state of eternal reward, no one can know the knowledge of God, which is unfamiliar to human minds, except the one who also receives the ability to possess it.[17]

From *Moralia* 19.2 [4], 9–17.
CCSL 143A: 958.

On Revelation 3.2: *Be watchful and strengthen the things that remain, which are on the point of death, for I do not find your works complete in the sight of God.*

6. It is said by Solomon: "He who is feeble and lax in his own work is akin to him who squanders his own works."[18] For clearly he who does not meticulously persevere in the good works he has begun imitates through his careless laxity the hand of the destroyer. For this reason it is said by the angel to the church of Sardis: *Be watchful and strengthen the things that remain, which are on the point of death, for I do not find your works complete in the sight of God* (Rv 3.2). So then, because his works had not been found complete in the sight of God, he predicted that those [works] which remained, even those which had been done, were on the point of death. For if that which is dead within us is not roused to life, even that which is held onto as if still alive will be extinguished.

From *Book on Pastoral Care* 3.34,
85–96. SC 382: 508–10.

17. The final sentence here varies in the manuscripts, no doubt because of some primitive corruption in the transmission of the text. The version followed here reflects the reading of the CCSL edition. The PL version of this sentence (PL 79: 1109b) differs somewhat from the CCSL version: "But to possess a new name written on a stone is to possess, in a state of eternal reward, the knowledge of God unfamiliar to human minds, which no one can know except him who also receives it."

18. Prv 18.9.

On Revelation 3.12: *He who conquers, I will make him a pillar in the temple of God.*

7. *He who conquers, I will make him a pillar in the temple of my God* (Rv 3.12). For anyone who is steadfast with the right intention in the work of God is set up as a pillar in the structure of the spiritual edifice, so that, placed in this temple, which is the Church, he may provide both usefulness and adornment.

From *Moralia* 17.39 [42], 6–9.
CCSL 143A: 875.

On Revelation 3.15–16: *Would that you were cold or hot! But because you are lukewarm, and neither cold nor hot, I am going to spew you out of my mouth.*

8. *Would that you were cold or hot! But because you are lukewarm, and neither cold nor hot, I am going to spew you out of my mouth* (Rv 3.15–16). Indeed, one is hot who takes on and completes good works, but one is cold who does not even begin the works he ought to complete. And just as one passes from cold to hot by going through lukewarmness, so too one returns from hot to cold by going through lukewarmness. Therefore, whoever lives having lost the coldness of unbelief, but without progressing further by overcoming lukewarmness to become hot with fervor, unquestionably acts to regain his coldness, having despaired of becoming hot while lingering in harmful lukewarmness. But just as he who is cold has hope in anticipation of being lukewarm, so too he who has grown lukewarm after being cold despairs. For he who is still in sin does not lose confidence in being converted, but he who grows lukewarm after his conversion also loses the hope that is possible for the cold sinner. Therefore, each person is required to be either hot or cold, lest, being lukewarm, he be spewed out. That is to say, while not yet converted he should still hold onto the hope of being converted, or, if already converted, he should burn brightly with the virtues, lest being lukewarm he be spewed out, because through his apathy he returns from the hotness, in which he began, to harmful coldness.

From *Book on Pastoral Care* 3.34,
102–120. SC 382: 510.

On Revelation 3.17: *You say, "I am rich," and "I have prospered," and "I need nothing," and you do not realize that you are wretched, pitiable, poor, naked, and blind.*

9. By the voice of the angel it is said to the preacher of Laodicea: *You say, "I am rich," and "I have prospered," and "I need nothing," and you do not realize that you are wretched, pitiable, poor, naked, and blind* (Rv 3.17). He who proudly exalts himself because of his sanctity declares himself, as it were, to be rich, but is proved to be poor, blind, and naked: poor, assuredly, because he lacks the richness of virtues; blind, because he fails to see the poverty that he suffers; naked, because he lost his first garment—no, even worse, because he does not even realize that he has lost it.

> From *Moralia* 34.3 [6], 33–41.
> CCSL 143B: 1736.

On Revelation 3.18: *I counsel you to buy refined gold from me.*

10. But what does he call gold, if not wisdom? For this is what is said about it by Solomon: "A desirable treasure rests in the mouth of the wise man."[19] Surely, it is because he sees wisdom as gold, which he called a treasure. It is also rightly signified by the name "gold" because, just as gold purchases temporal goods, so too wisdom eternal goods. If wisdom were not gold, it would never have been said by the angel to the church of Laodicea: *I counsel you to buy refined gold from me* (Rv 3.18). For we buy gold when, about to receive wisdom, we first pay obedience. And it is clearly this transaction that a certain wise man intently urges us to make, saying: "If you desire wisdom, keep the commandments, and the Lord will grant it to you."[20]

> From *Moralia* 4.31 [61], 7–17.
> CCSL 143: 205–6.

On Revelation 3.18: *Anoint your eyes with salve, that you may see.*

11. It is said by the angel: *Anoint your eyes with salve, that you may see* (Rv 3.18). For we anoint our eyes with salve that we may see when,

19. Prv 21.20.
20. Sir 1.33.

in order to comprehend the brightness of the true light, we help the vision of our intellect by applying the medicine of [good] works.

From *Book on Pastoral Care* 1.11,
67–71. SC 381: 168.

On Revelation 3.21: *He who conquers, I will grant him to sit with me on my throne, as I myself conquered and sat with my Father on his throne.*

12. Now holy men are rightly called "kings," according to the testimony of sacred Scripture, because they have been raised above all the motions of the flesh: now they control the appetite for over-indulgence, now they cool the heat of greed, now they bow down the boastfulness of pride, now they crush the suggestion of envy, now they quench the fire of rage. They are kings, then, because they have learned not to succumb to the motions of their temptations by consenting to them but to gain the mastery by ruling over them. So then, because they pass from this power of ruling to the power of rewarding what is due, let it be rightly said: "He places kings on the throne forever."[21] For by ruling over themselves they are wearied for a time, but they are placed forever on the throne of the kingdom of internal elevation, and there they learn to judge others as they deserve, just as here they never learned to go easy on themselves when they did not deserve it. For thus it is said in another place: "Until righteousness is turned into judgment."[22] And Paul says of himself and his associates: "So that in him we might become the righteousness of God."[23] Righteousness, then, is turned into judgment because those who now live righteously and irreproachably will then obtain the power to judge others. Hence the Lord said to the church of Laodicea: *He who conquers, I will grant him to sit with me on my throne, as I myself conquered and sat with my Father on his throne* (Rv 3.21). The Lord declares that he sat as a conqueror with the Father on his throne because after the struggles of the passion, after the victory of the resurrection, he showed more clearly to all that he was equal to the power of the Father and made it known that he was not unequal to him by having trampled underfoot the

---

21. Jb 36.7.
22. Ps 93.15. Psalm numbering is according to the LXX.
23. 2 Cor 5.21.

sting of death.[24] Thus he also says to Mary, who still did not believe that he was like the Father: "Do not touch me, for I have not yet ascended to the Father."[25] Now for us, sitting on the throne of the Son means judging with the authority of the selfsame Son. After all, it is because we have received the right to judge from his own power that we sit, as it were, on his throne. Nor is it inconsistent with the truth that he testifies in other places that the disciples will sit on twelve thrones,[26] while here he asserts that they will sit upon his throne. For by the twelve thrones is indicated the universal judgment, but by the throne of the Son the special preeminence of judicial power. One and the same thing, then, is designated by twelve thrones and by the single throne of the Son, because clearly universal judgment is undertaken by the intervention of our Mediator.

From *Moralia* 26.28 [53], 15–50.
CCSL 143B: 1307–8.

On Revelation 4.10: *And they worshiped him who lives forever, casting their crowns before the throne.*

13. Now holy men know that they are sprung from a corruptible stock from the time of the fall of our first parent, and that not by their own virtue but by grace from above coming first to them[27] they are changed to better inclinations and works. And whatever evil they detect in themselves they realize is the desert of their mortal descent; but whatever good they see in themselves they recognize as a gift of immortal grace. And because of this gift received they become debtors to him who, by coming first to them,[28] gave them the will to do the good that they did not will, and, by going to them subsequently, granted them the ability to do the good that they willed. Hence it is well said by John: *And they worshiped him who lives forever, casting their crowns before the throne of the Lord* (Rv 4.10). For to cast their crowns before the throne is to attribute victories in their conflicts not to themselves but to their Author, so as to refer

24. Cf. 1 Cor 15.56.
25. Jn 20.17.
26. Cf. Lk 22.30; Mt 19.28.
27. Lat. *preveniente superna gratia*, which could also be translated "prevenient grace from above."
28. Lat. *praeveniendo*. See note above.

the glory of praise to him from whom they know that they have
received the powers for the conflict.

From *Moralia* 22.9 [20], 13–26.
CCSL 143A: 1107–8.

On Revelation 6.9–11: *I saw under the altar the souls of those who had been
slain for the word of God and for the witness they had borne. And they cried
out with a great voice: "How long, O Lord, holy and true, before you judge and
avenge our blood on those who dwell upon the earth?" White robes were given
to each, and it was said to them that they should rest still a little longer, until
the number of their fellow servants and brothers should be complete.*

14. It is said in the Apocalypse of John: *I saw under the altar the
souls of those who had been slain for the word of God and for the witness they
had borne. And they cried out with a great voice: "How long, O Lord, holy and
true, before you judge and avenge our blood on those who dwell upon the earth?"*
(Rv 6.9–10). Then in the same place it is added: *White robes were given
to each, and it was said to them that they should rest still a little longer, until
the number of their fellow servants and brothers should be complete* (Rv 6.11).
What does it mean for souls to utter a petition for vengeance, if not
to desire the day of final judgment and the resurrection of lifeless
bodies? And indeed, the greatness of their cry indicates the greatness of their desire. For the less one desires, the less one cries out.
And the more complete is the pouring out of oneself in desire for
the unbounded Spirit, the more loudly the voice sounds in his ears.
And so, the words of souls are their very desires. For if speech were
not desire, the prophet would not have said: "Your ear has heard
the desire of their heart."[29] But as the mind that petitions is usually
disposed in one way and the mind that is petitioned in another, and
yet the souls of the saints cling to God in the bosom of their inner-
most secrecy in such a way that in clinging they find rest, how are
they said to petition, seeing that it seems they never diverge in any
way from his internal will? How can they be said to petition, seeing
that it is certain they are not ignorant both of the will of God and
of those things that shall be? But being so rooted in him, they are
said to petition something from him, not because they desire anything that is out of harmony with the will of him whom they know,

29. Ps 9.38 (LXX).

but because the greater the ardor with which they cling to him, the more they also receive from him the ability to petition from him that which they know he wants them to do. And so, they drink from him that which they thirst after from him. And in a way still incomprehensible to us, by foreknowledge they are satisfied with that which they hunger for by petitioning. So then, they would be out of harmony with their Creator's will if they did not petition for what they see him willing, and they would cling less closely to him if, when he wants to bestow, they knocked with reluctant desire.[30] To them this response is given by God: *Rest still a little longer, until the number of your fellow servants and brothers should be complete* (Rv 6.11).[31] To say "rest still a little longer" to these desiring souls is amid their burning desires to breathe upon them the soothings of consolation by means of foreknowledge itself, so that the voice of their souls is the desire roused in them through love, and the word of God in response is that he reassures them amid their desires with the certainty of satisfaction. So then, his response that they ought to await the gathering of their brothers is his imparting to their minds the delays of cheerful waiting, so that, as they long for the resurrection of the flesh, they may also be gladdened by an increased number of brothers who should be gathered to them.

From *Moralia* 2.7 [11], 64–105.
CCSL 143: 66–67.

On Revelation 6.11: *White robes were given to each, and it was said to them that they should rest still a little longer, until the number of their fellow servants and brothers should be complete.*

15. For the holy Church to receive double at her end is for her to rejoice over every single one of us in our blessedness of soul and incorruptibility of flesh.[32] Now it is for this reason that it is said about the elect by the prophet: "They shall possess double in their land."[33] And for this reason too, the apostle John said about the

30. Cf. Mt 7.7-8; Lk 11.9-10.
31. Note that Gregory has changed the indirect speech into direct speech.
32. In its original context, this excerpt immediately follows Gregory's first interpretation of Jb 42.10: *The Lord gave Job double of what he had before.* The excerpt here is his second interpretation.
33. Is 61.7.

saints who were seeking the end of the world: *White robes were given to each, and it was said to them that they should rest still a little longer, until the number of their fellow servants and brothers should be complete* (Rv 6.11). [For as we said far above,][34] before the resurrection[35] the saints each receive a single robe because they enjoy only the blessedness of their souls, but at the end of the world they will be clothed in two robes because along with their blessedness of mind they shall also possess the glory of the flesh.

> From *Moralia* 35.13 [25], 28–39.
> CCSL 143: 1789–90.

On Revelation 6.12: *The sun became as sackcloth.*

16. Sometimes in sacred Scripture the brightness of preachers is designated by the term "sun." And so it is said by John: *The sun became as sackcloth* (Rv 6.12). For in the last days the sun looks like sackcloth because the shining life of preachers appears before the eyes of the reprobate as harsh and contemptible.

> From *Moralia* 9.8 [8], 2–7.
> CCSL 143: 460–61.

---

34. Cf. *Moralia* Praef. 10 [20], 1-22 (CCSL 143: 23): "It is a good that after Job's loss of his possessions, after his children's deaths, after the excruciating pain of his wounds, after his verbal contests and battles, he is raised up again with a double reward, because the holy Church, even while still in this present life, receives a double recompense for the toils she undergoes. For after taking in the Gentiles to the full, at the end of the world she also converts to herself the souls of the Jews. Now it is for this reason that it is written: *Until the full number of the Gentiles come in, and so all Israel will be saved* (Rom 11.25- 26). And she will afterwards receive a double recompense because when the toil of this present time is finished, she ascends not only to the joy of souls but also to the beatitude of bodies. And hence it is rightly said through the prophet: *They shall possess double in their land* (Is 61.7). For in the land of the living (cf. Ps 26.13, etc.) the saints possess double because surely they rejoice in beatitude of both mind and body. Hence John in the Apocalypse, because it was before the resurrection of bodies that he saw the souls of the saints crying out, beheld how they each had received a single stole, saying: *White robes were given to each, and it was said to them that they should rest still a little longer, until the number of their fellow servants and brothers should be complete* (Rv 6.11). For before the resurrection they are each said to have received a single stole because they still enjoy only the beatitude of their mind. So then, they will each receive two robes when along with the perfect joy of their souls they shall also be clothed with the incorruptibility of their bodies."

35. I.e., the final resurrection.

On Revelation 7.9–10: *With palm branches in their hands they indeed cry out with a great voice, saying: "Salvation to our God who sits upon the throne and to the Lamb!"*

17. What is designated by palm branches, if not the rewards of victory? Indeed, it is the custom to give them to victors. And so, those who had conquered the ancient enemy in the battle of martyrdom are now rejoicing as victors in the [heavenly] homeland. It is written: *With palm branches in their hands they indeed cry out with a great voice, saying: "Salvation to our God who sits upon the throne and to the Lamb!"* (Rv 7.9–10). For to hold palm branches in the hands is to have gained victories through good effort. The palm branch for this good effort is bestowed in the place where there is now rejoicing without combat.

From *Homilies on Ezekiel* 2.5 [22],
546–53. CCSL 143: 291.

On Revelation 8.1: *There was silence in heaven for about half an hour.*

18. Solitude of mind is rightly granted to those of good conduct, that they may keep down the din of earthly desires rising within; that they may restrain by the grace of heavenly love the troubles of heart which bubble up from the depths; and that they may swat away from the eyes of the mind with the hand of seriousness all motions of trivial thoughts which importunely present themselves, as if they were flies flitting around; in order that they may seek for themselves some secret abode with the Lord within themselves where they may, once the exterior clamor has ceased, speak silently with him by their inward desires. It is said elsewhere of this secret abode of the heart: *There was silence in heaven for about half an hour* (Rv 8.1). For the Church of the elect is called "heaven," which, as she stretches toward the [eternal] heights through the elevation of contemplation, keeps down the tumult of thoughts surging up from the depths and makes a kind of silent abode for God within herself. Since indeed this silence of contemplation cannot be perfect in this life, it is said to last for about half an hour. For since the tumultuous clamor of thoughts forces itself into the soul against its will, it violently drags the eye of the heart, even when stretching toward the heights, back down to the consideration of earthly things. And so, it is written: "The body that is corruptible weighs down the soul, and

the earthly habitation burdens the mind thinking many things."[36]
So then, this silence is well described as lasting not for a whole but
for a half hour, because contemplation is never perfected here, however ardently it be begun.

From *Moralia* 30.16 [52–53], 9–32.
CCSL 143B: 1527.

19. *There was silence in heaven for about half an hour* (Rv 8.1). For the
soul of a righteous person is "heaven," as the Lord said through
the prophet: "Heaven is my throne."[37] And: "The heavens declare
the glory of God."[38] So then, when the stillness of the contemplative life is settled in the mind, there is silence in heaven, because the
clamor of earthly activities recedes from thought, so that the soul
inclines to the secret internal ear. But because this stillness of mind
cannot be perfect in this life, it is not said that the silence in heav-
en lasts for a whole hour but *for about half an hour.* And not even an
exact half hour is fully measured since an "about" is added. For as
soon as the soul begins to elevate itself and be bathed with the light
of interior stillness, the clamor of thoughts swiftly returns, and the
soul becomes confused about itself and in its confusion is blinded.

From *Homilies on Ezekiel* 2.2 [14],
353–365. CCSL 142: 235.

On Revelation 9.19: *The power of horses was in their mouth and in their
tails.*
20. And so, what will be that time of persecution when some rage
with words, others with swords, to destroy the piety of the faithful?[39]
For that which is said to them by some with enticing words is en-
forced by others with swinging swords. The conduct of both, that

36. Wis 9.15.
37. Is 66.1.
38. Ps 18.1.
39. At this point the excerpter omits the following lines: "For what person, even
if weak, would not despise the teeth of Leviathan, if terror did not defend them
[the teeth] by a circle of worldly powers? But they are proceeded against with a
double cunning." Since this excerpt is taken from Gregory's interpretation of Jb
41.5, *In a circle is the terror of his teeth*, these lines, which refer to this verse, were probably omitted as not relevant to Gregory's exposition of Rv 9.19.

is, of the enforcers and the enticers, is summed up in the Apocalypse of John in a brief sentence, which says: *The power of horses was in their mouth and in their tails* (Rv 9.19). For the "mouth" figuratively represents the knowledge that belongs to teachers, whereas the "tail" the power that belongs to worldly men. Indeed, by the "tail," which is behind, is designated the transitory nature of this world that will be left behind, about which the Apostle Paul says: "One thing I do, forgetting what lies behind and straining forward to what lies ahead."[40] For everything that passes away is behind, whereas everything that comes and remains is ahead. So then, the power of these horses, that is, of those most wicked preachers who hasten everywhere by carnal impulse, is in their mouth and in their tail. For they themselves indeed preach perverse things with persuasive discourses, but, relying as they do upon temporal powers, they exalt themselves by means of those things which are behind. And because there is the possibility of appearing despicable, they demand respect to be given to them from their evil hearers, by means of those on whose patronage they rely.

From *Moralia* 33.27 [48], 25–46.
CCSL 143B: 1715.


On Revelation 10.4: *Seal up what the seven thunders have said.*

21. For indeed when the end of the world is impending, heavenly knowledge improves and grows greater with time. Now for this reason it is said by Daniel: "Many shall run to and fro, and knowledge shall be increased."[41] And for this reason too, the angel says to John in the first part of the revelation: *Seal up what the seven thunders have said* (Rv 10.4). And yet at the end of the same revelation he commands him: *Do not seal the words of the prophecy in this book* (Rv 22.10). Now the first part of the revelation is commanded to be sealed up, but the sealing up of the end is forbidden, because whatever was hidden at the beginnings of the holy Church the end reveals day by day.

From *Moralia* 9.11 [15], 92–100.
CCSL 143: 467.

40. Phil 3.13.
41. Dn 12.4. Gregory neglects to quote the first part of Dn 12.4, *But you, Daniel, shut up the words and seal up the book, until the time of the end,* whose wording may have led him to connect it with the two passages from the Apocalypse cited in this excerpt.

On Revelation 11.2: *The court that is outside the temple, cast out; do not measure it.*

22. In the Apocalypse it is written: *The court that is outside the temple, cast out; do not measure it* (Rv 11.2). For what does the "court" signify other than the wideness of the present life? And those designated by the term "court" are rightly outside the temple and accordingly not to be measured, because "narrow is the gate that leads to life,"[42] and thus the wideness of the life of the depraved prohibits entry into the measures and rules of the elect.

From Moralia 28.6 [16], 24–30.<br>CCSL 143B: 1407.

On Revelation 11.4: *These are the two olive trees and the two lampstands standing in the sight of the Lord of the earth.*

23. Those two illustrious preachers were taken away but not before their deaths were delayed, so that they might be brought back at the end to deliver useful preaching. About them it is said by John: *These are the two olive trees and the two lampstands standing in the sight of the Lord of the earth* (Rv 11.4). One of them is promised in the Gospel through the Truth himself, saying: "Elijah is to come, and he will restore all things."[43]

From Moralia 9.8 [9], 43–48.<br>CCSL 143: 462.

On Revelation 12.1: *A woman clothed with the sun and with the moon under her feet.*

24. When the sun is used figuratively [in Scripture], sometimes it designates the Lord, sometimes persecution, sometimes the manifestation of the clear sight of something, but sometimes the understanding of the wise. Now by the "sun" the Lord is figuratively represented as when in the Book of Wisdom it is testified that all the impious on the day of final judgment will say in full knowledge of their own damnation: "We strayed from the way of truth, and the light of righteousness did not shine upon us, and the sun did not

---

42. Mt 7.14.

43. Mt 17.11. The other preacher taken away before death who will return at the end is Enoch.

rise upon us."[44] It is as if they were saying in plain speech: "The ray of inward light did not shine upon us." In a similar manner, John said: *A woman clothed with the sun and with the moon under her feet* (Rv 12.1). For by the "sun" is understood the illumination of truth, whereas by the "moon," which wanes when the month is completed, the changeableness of temporal existence. But because the holy Church is protected by the splendor of light from above, she is, as it were, clothed with the sun. But because she despises all temporal things, she tramples the moon under her feet.

From *Moralia* 34.14 [25], 1–15.
CCSL 143B: 1750.

On Revelation 12.4: *The dragon put forth his tail and swept away a third part of the stars and cast them onto the earth.*

25. [In sacred Scripture] by the word "stars" is sometimes indicated the righteousness of the saints, which shines in the darkness of this life, but sometimes the false pretense of hypocrites, who display the good they do to win praise from men. For if those who live rightly were not stars, Paul would never have said to his disciples: "In the midst of a depraved and perverse generation, among whom you shine as lights in the world."[45] And again, among those who appear to live rightly, if some of them were not seeking by their actions the reward of human esteem, John would never have seen stars falling from the heavens and said: *The dragon put forth his tail and swept away a third part of the stars* (Rv 12.4). For a part of the stars is swept away by the dragon's tail, because, in Antichrist's final attempts at seduction, certain ones who appear to shine will be snatched away. Now to sweep away stars onto the earth is, through the love of earthly things, to entangle in the wickedness of open error those who appear to be devoted to the pursuit of the heavenly life.

From *Moralia* 4.10 [17], 1–16.
CCSL 143: 174–75.

44. Wis 5.6.
45. Phil 2.15.

26. It is said by John about this tail of the Behemoth[46] in the form
of the dragon: *And his tail swept away a third part of the stars and cast
them onto the earth* (Rv 12.4). Now "heaven"[47] is the Church, which
in this night of the present life contains within herself the countless
virtues of the saints and so shines from above with radiant stars.
But the tail of the dragon casts the stars down upon the earth, because that extremity of Satan, which is raised up through the bold-
ness of the person it has taken hold of, gains possession of some
whom it finds in the Church appearing to be the elect of God and
by this unmasks them as reprobates. And so, for the stars to fall
from heaven onto the earth is for some, having abandoned hope for
heavenly things, to long, under his guidance, for the ostentation of
worldly glory.

From *Moralia* 32.15 [25], 91–101.
CCSL 143B: 1648–49.

On Revelation 12.7: *War arose with Michael the archangel.*

27. Now "Michael" [means], "Who is like God?"[48] And as often
as anything is done with amazing power, Michael is said to be sent,
so that from his very feat and name it may be given to understand
that no one can do what God can do. And so, that ancient enemy who desired to be like God through pride said: "I will ascend
into heaven; above the stars of heaven I will raise up my throne; I
will sit on the mountain of testimony on the slopes of the north; I
will ascend above the height of the clouds; I will be like the Most
High."[49] At the end of the world, his power is relinquished to him
even though he is on the verge of being destroyed in the final punishment. For he is said to be heading for battle with the archangel Michael, as is said by John: *War arose with Michael the archangel*
(Rv 12.7), so that he who proudly exalted himself to the likeness of

46. This excerpt is taken from Gregory's commentary on Jb 40.15-24, which
deals with the Behemoth.

47. Cf. Rv 12.3, which describes the portent as appearing *in heaven.*

48. This is the meaning of "Michael" in Hebrew, a fact often mentioned by the
Church fathers. At this point the excerpter omits, "'Gabriel' means 'strength of
God,' and 'Raphael' 'healing of God,'" no doubt because these lines were considered irrelevant for the excerpt. As was the case with "Michael," the Church fathers
frequently pointed out these Hebrew etymologies of "Gabriel" and "Raphael."

49. Is 14.13-14.

God may learn, once he has been destroyed by Michael, that no one rises up to the likeness of God through pride.

From *Homilies on the Gospels* 34 [9],
199–212. CCSL 141: 307.

On Revelation 12.10: *For the accuser of our brothers has been cast down, who day and night accused them before God.*

28. The crafty adversary, when he observes your offspring living well in prosperity, hastens by means of adversity to prove him to be reprobate before the judge. And so, it is rightly said by the voice of the angel in the Apocalypse: *For the accuser of our brothers has been cast down, who day and night accused them before our God* (Rv 12.10). Now sacred Scripture is accustomed to put "day" for prosperity and "night" for adversity. So then, he does not stop accusing us day and night, because in times of both prosperity and adversity he endeavors to show that we are worthy of accusation. He accuses in the day when he insinuates that we abuse prosperity. He accuses in the night when he shows that we lack patience in adversity.

From *Moralia* 2.9 [15], 9–19.
CCSL 143: 69.

On Revelation 13.11: *I saw another beast arising from the earth with two horns like a lamb, and he spoke like a dragon.*

29. *I saw another beast arising from the earth with two horns like a lamb, and he spoke like a dragon* (Rv 13.11). In a previous description already given above, he told of the first beast, that is, Antichrist.[50] After him this other beast is said to have arisen, because in the wake of Antichrist the multitude of his preachers boasts of his earthly power. For to arise from the earth is to swell with the pride of earthly glory. This [beast] has two horns like a lamb, because the wisdom and conduct which the Lord truly and uniquely possessed in himself, this beast, through a pretense of holiness, falsely asserts are present in himself. But because the poison of serpents is poured into the ears of his reprobate hearers under the appearance of the lamb, it is rightly added there: *And he spoke like a dragon* (Rv 13.11). So then, if that beast, that is, the multitude of his preachers, were to speak

---

50. Gregory is probably referring to Rv 12.3-4.

openly like a dragon, he would not appear like a lamb. But he takes
on the appearance of a lamb in order to do the works of a dragon.

From *Moralia* 33.35 [59], 10–24.
CCSL 143B: 1724.

On Revelation 12.12: *Woe to you, O earth and sea! For the devil has come
down to you with great wrath, knowing that his time is short!*

30. As the age of the world increases with each coming year, it
is disturbed by more frequent evils; and as it receives an increase
of age, it feels the loss of its health. For its troubles increase along
with its years; and it bears losses in life with less fortitude, the more
it continues to advance, as it were, to life.[51] For the ancient enemy
is loosed against it with all his strength; although at present he has
already perished because he has lost the blessedness of his heavenly
condition, yet at that time[52] he is more fully extinguished when he
is divested of his license to tempt and is bound fast in eternal fires.
And so, at the end of the world he draws near intending to tempt
with greater severity, because he becomes more fervent in his cruelty the more he senses that he is closer to punishment. For he real-
izes that he is on the verge of losing his license of the wickedest sort
of autonomy; and the more he is constrained by the shortness of the
time, the more he proliferates himself in numerous acts of cruelty,
as is said of him by the voice of the angel to John: *Woe to you, O earth
and sea! For the devil has come down to you with great wrath, knowing that his
time is short!* (Rv 12.12). So then, at that time he expands himself to
a fervor of great wrath, as he who could not remain in blessedness
attempts to avoid falling into the pit of damnation with the few. At
that time whatever power of evildoing he possesses he seeks to use
with greater cunning. At that time he exalts more highly his neck of
pride. And by means of that damned man to whom he gives birth
he displays with wicked intent all the temporal power he possesses.

From *Moralia* 34.1 [1], 8–29.
CCSL 143B: 1733.

51. I.e., to eternal life. Gregory compares the world advancing to its end to a
human being growing old, dying, and gaining eternal life.
52. I.e., at the end of the world.

On Revelation 13.13: *So that he made fire come down from heaven.*

31. For at that time every soul is like a boiling pot, enduring the vehemence of its own thoughts as if it were the foam of scalding waves, which both the fire of zeal sets in motion and temporal oppressiveness itself keeps confined within like a pot.[53] And so, John too, when telling of the portents of this beast, added: *So that he made fire come down from heaven* (Rv 13.13). Indeed, for fire to come down from heaven is for flames of holy zeal to shoot out from the heavenly regions into the souls of the elect.

From *Moralia* 33.37 [62], 2–9.
CCSL 143B: 1727.

On Revelation 14.4: *These are the ones who have not defiled themselves with women, for they are virgins; they follow the Lamb wherever he goes.*

32. It is said by John: *These are the ones who have not defiled themselves with women, for they are virgins; they follow the Lamb wherever he goes* (Rv 14.4). And they sing a song that no one can sing, except the one hundred forty-four thousand.[54] For indeed to sing a song to the Lamb by oneself is to rejoice with him forever over the incorruptibility of the flesh in the presence of all the faithful. But the rest of the elect are able to hear this song, even though they cannot sing it. For charity leads them to rejoice in the loftiness of the others,[55] even though they do not rise up to the others' level of distinction.

From *Book on Pastoral Care* 3.28,
95–104. SC 382: 462–64.

On Revelation 14.14: *I looked, and behold! a white cloud, and upon the cloud sat one like a son of a man, having a golden crown on his head and a sharp sickle in his hand.*

33. *I looked, and behold! a white cloud, and upon the cloud sat one like a son of a man, having a golden crown on his head and a sharp sickle in his hand* (Rv 14.14). For the power of the divine judgment is called a "ring,"

53. Here Gregory is commenting on Jb 41.11, *Like a boiling and burning pot.*
54. Cf. Rv 14.3.
55. I.e., the virgins whom Gregory identifies with the one hundred forty-four thousand.

because it holds one in at every point.[56] But because it captures everything within its embrace by cutting, it is also signified by the designation "sickle." For whatever is cut by a sickle falls inward, in whatever direction it is turned. And because the power of the judgment from on high can never be avoided (we are indeed within its embrace, however much we try to escape it), when the judge who is to come appears, he is rightly said to have a sickle, because when he comes to meet all things in his might, he encircles them by cutting them. The prophet saw that he was within the embrace of the sickle of judgment when he said: "If I go up to heaven, you are there; if I go down to hell, you are there; if I take the wings of the dawn, and dwell at the sea's furthest end, even there your hand would lead me and your right hand hold me fast."[57] He saw himself within the embrace of a kind of sickle, when he realized that there was no way of escape open to him from any place, saying: "For neither from the east, nor from the west, nor from the desert mountains"[58]—"is there a way of escape open" being understood. And immediately he proceeds to the all-embracing comprehension of the power from on high, saying: "For God is the judge."[59] It is as if he were saying: "A way of escape is nowhere to be found, because he who judges is everywhere."

> From *Moralia* 33.11 [21], 18–38.
> CCSL 143B: 1691.

On Revelation 21.18: *The city itself was pure gold, clear as glass.*

34. By the term "gold" is understood the splendor of the heavenly city, as when John testifies that he saw it, saying: *The city itself was pure gold, clear as glass* (Rv 21.18). Now the gold, of which that [city] consists, is said to be like glass, so that both by the gold may be designated its brightness and by the glass its clearness. And again, by the term "gold" is suggested charity, as when the same John beheld the angel speaking with him having a golden girdle around

---

56. Gregory is commenting on Jb 40.21, *Can you put a ring in his nose?*
57. Ps 138.8-10.
58. Ps 74.7.
59. Ps 74.8.

his breast.[60] For surely, insofar as the breasts of the citizens of heaven are no longer subjected to the fear of punishment and are not divided from each other by any dissension, they bind themselves together by charity alone. For to have a golden girdle around the breast is to bind together all the movements of our unstable thoughts through the bonds of love alone.

From *Moralia* 34.15 [26], 5–22.
CCSL 143B: 1752.

On Revelation 16.8: *The fourth angel poured forth his vial on the sun, and it was granted him to afflict human beings with heat and fire.*

35. By the term "sun" is expressed the understanding of the wise, as is written in the Apocalypse: *The fourth angel poured forth his vial on the sun, and it was granted him to afflict human beings with heat and fire* (Rv 16.8). Clearly, to pour a vial on the sun is to inflict the punishments of persecution upon men[61] who shine with the splendor of wisdom. *And it was granted him to afflict human beings with heat and fire.* For when wise men[62] are overcome by tortures and stricken with the error of bad living, the weak are persuaded by their example and start to burn with desires for temporal goods. For the downfalls of the strong bring about increases in the destructions of the weak. That the keenness of the wise is designated by the sun is also said by way of a simile by Solomon: "A wise man remains like the sun; a foolish man will change like the moon."[63] So then, in this passage what is indicated by the rays of the sun, if not the keenness of the wise? For because many, who seemed to shine in the holy Church with the light of wisdom, when either caught by seductions, or terrified by threats, or broken down by tortures, submit themselves at that time to the rebellion of Leviathan, it is rightly said: "Under him will be the rays of the sun."[64] It is as if it were being said in plain speech: "These who within the holy Church seemed by the keenness of their wisdom to spread, as it were, rays of light, and by the author-

---

60. Cf. Rv 1.13; 15.6.
61. Lat. *viris.*
62. Lat. *viri.*
63. Sir 27.12.
64. Jb 41.21.

ity of their uprightness to shine from above, submit themselves to
the power of the Leviathan through their wicked deeds."[65]

> From *Moralia* 34.14 [25], 27–47.
> CCSL 143B: 1750–51.

On Revelation 16.15: *Blessed is he who is awake and keeps his garments,*
*lest he walk naked and they see his shame!*

36. For if in God's sight our works did not cover us like garments,
it would never have been said by the voice of the angel: *Blessed is he*
*who is awake and keeps his garments, lest he walk naked and they see his*
*shame!* (Rv 16.15). For our shame is detected precisely when our life
is judged blameworthy in the eyes of the righteous yet lacks the
covering of ensuing good work.

> From *Moralia* 2.51 [81], 2  8.
> CCSL 143: 108–9.

On Revelation 16.15: *Blessed is he who is awake and keeps his garments,*
*lest he walk naked!*

37. Just as garments protect the body, so too good works protect
the soul. And so, it is said to someone: *Blessed is he who is awake and*
*keeps his garments, lest he walk naked!* (Rv 16.15).

> From *Moralia* 16.50 [63], 2–5.
> CCSL 143A: 835.

On Revelation 17.15: *The waters that you saw are peoples.*

38. In sacred Scripture it is the custom for "peoples" to be designated by "waters." And so, it is said by John: *The waters are peoples*
(Rv 17.15). So then, a people is designated by waters, because in life
it has the sound of the tumult of the flesh and flows away each day
by the downward course of mortality.

> From *Homilies on Ezekiel* 1.8 [1], 5–8.
> CCSL 142: 101.

---

65. The excerpter, no doubt to eliminate the interpretation of Jb 41.21, short-
ened Gregory's lines after the citation of Sir 27.12 as follows: "So then, in this
passage what is indicated by the rays of the sun, if not the keenness of the wise,
who within the holy Church seemed by the keenness of their wisdom to spread, as
it were, rays of light, and by the authority of their uprightness to shine?"

On Revelation 19.9: *Blessed are those who are invited to the marriage supper of the Lamb.*

39. Therefore, concerning this final banquet, it is mentioned elsewhere by John: *Blessed are those who are invited to the marriage supper of the Lamb* (Rv 19.9). Now, then, he does not say they have been invited to a luncheon but to a supper, because surely a supper at the end of the day is a banquet. So then, when the course of the present life is complete, those who come to the refreshment of heavenly contemplation are not invited to the luncheon of the Lamb but rather to his supper.

From *Homilies on the Gospels* 24 [6],
150–155. CCSL 141: 202.

On Revelation 19.10: *See that you do not do that! I am your fellow servant and one of your brothers.*

40. Lot and Joshua worship angels and yet are not prohibited from worshiping them.[66] But in the Apocalypse John wants to worship an angel, and yet the same angel stops him from feeling obligated to worship him, saying: *See that you do not do that! I am your fellow servant and one of your brothers* (Rv 19.10). Why is it that before the advent of the Redeemer angels are worshiped by human beings and they remain silent, but afterwards they balk at being worshiped? It must be because after they behold our nature, which they formerly despised, taken up above themselves, they become fearful of seeing it placed beneath themselves. No longer did they dare to scorn as beneath themselves and weak what they venerate above themselves, namely, in the King of heaven. Nor do they disdain having a human being as their companion, seeing that they worship the God-man above themselves.

From *Homilies on the Gospels* 8 [2],
45–58. CCSL 141: 55–56.

On Revelation 19.14: *And the armies that are in heaven were following him on white horses.*

41. Now the horse[67] is each holy soul's very own body, which

---

66. Cf. Gn 19.1; Jos 5.13–15.

67. Here Gregory is commenting on Jb 39.18, *When the time comes, she raises her wings on high; she laughs at the horse and his rider.*

clearly it knows how to restrain from unlawful pursuits by the bridle of self-control and again to let loose in the performance of good works by the goad of charity. And so, the apostle John too, in the Apocalypse, after he contemplated the Lord, said: *And the armies that are in heaven were following him on white horses* (Rv 19.14). For the multitude of the saints who had toiled in this war of martyrdom he rightly calls an "army." And for this reason they are said to be sitting upon white horses, because surely their bodies shone brilliantly with both the light of righteousness and the whiteness of purity.

> From *Moralia* 31.15 [27], 11–21.
> CCSL 143B: 1569–70.

On Revelation 19.16: *He had this written on his robe and on his thigh: King of kings and Lord of lords.*

42. It is said by John: *He had this written on his robe and on his thigh: King of kings and Lord of lords* (Rv 19.16). Now what is his robe, if not the body that he assumed from the Virgin? And yet his body is not one thing and he himself another thing.[68] For the flesh is also called our robe, but yet we ourselves are the flesh in which we are clothed. But long ago Isaiah gazed upon this robe of his as it bled with the blood of his suffering through the cross, saying: "Why is your garment red, and your robes like those of ones who tread in the winepress?"[69] And in reply he said to him: "I trod the winepress alone, and from the nations there is no one with me."[70] For he who trod alone the winepress in which he had been trodden is the one who by his own power is victorious over the suffering he endured. Indeed, he who suffered "even unto the death of the cross"[71] rose from death with glory. And it is well said: "And from the nations

---

68. Lat. *Quid enim uestimentum eius est, nisi corpus quod assumpsit ex uirgine? Nec tamen aliud eius uestimentum est, atque aliud ipse.* The excerpter, or a copyist, appears to have conflated these two sentences, by accidentally skipping from the first *uestimentum* to the second: *Quid enim eius uestimentum est, atque aliud ipse.* Here Gregory is careful to affirm the single subjectivity of Christ, in line with Chalcedonian Christology, lest he seem to be espousing a kind of Christological dualism, such as was associated with Nestorius.

69. Is 63.2.

70. Is 63.3.

71. Phil 2.8.

there is no one with me."[72] For those for whom he came to suffer ought to have been sharers in his suffering: because they did not yet at that time believe, in his suffering he lamented those whose life he sought in that suffering. But the propagation of the flesh takes place through the thigh. So then, because by means of the propagation of the human race, as Matthew and Luke narrate in their genealogies, he came into this world from the Virgin, and because by the mystery of his Incarnation he indicated to all peoples everywhere that he was King and Lord, he had this written on his robe and on his thigh: "King of kings and Lord of lords." For that means by which he made himself known to the world is the very means by which he implanted a knowledge of the Scriptures about himself.[73]

> From *Homilies on Ezekiel* 2.1 [9],
> 288–312. CCSL 142: 215.

On Revelation 20.1–3: *I saw an angel coming down from heaven, holding the key of the bottomless pit and a great chain in his hand. And he seized the dragon, that ancient serpent, who is the Devil and Satan, and bound him for a thousand years, and cast him into the bottomless pit, and shut it, and sealed it over him so that he would not deceive the nations any longer, until the thousand years were fulfilled.*

43. This Leviathan[74] the spirits of the elect angels imprisoned, shutting him up in the depths of the bottomless pit. And so, it is written: *I saw an angel coming down from heaven, holding the key of the bottomless pit and a great chain in his hand. And he seized the dragon, that ancient serpent, who is the Devil and Satan, and bound him for a thousand years, and cast him into the bottomless pit* (Rv 20.1–3). Yet at the end of the world they call him back for more open conflicts and let him completely loose against us with his powers. And so, it is again written in that same place: *And when the thousand years are completed, Satan will be released* (Rv 20.7). For that apostate angel, who was so created that he would be renowned among the other legions of angels, sank so low by his rising up in pride that now he lies prostrate under the authority of the angels who stand firm. For either he lies hidden at

---

72. Is 63.3.

73. Lat. *Unde enim in mundo innotuit, ibi de se lectionis scientiam infixit.*

74. Gregory is commenting on Jb 3.8, *Let those curse it who curse the day, who are ready to rouse up the Leviathan.*

the present time, bound by these angels in charge of him for our benefit, or he exerts himself against us with all his power at that time, released by those same angels who let him loose in order to test us.

From *Moralia* 4.9 [16], 55–69.
CCSL 143: 174.

44. *I saw an angel coming down from heaven, holding the key of the bottomless pit and a great chain in his hand. And he seized the dragon, that ancient serpent, who is the Devil and Satan, and bound him for a thousand years, and cast him into the bottomless pit, and shut it, and sealed it over him so that he would not deceive the nations any longer, until the thousand years were fulfilled* (Rv 20.1–3). Now by the number "thousand" he does not designate a length of time but the universality with which the Church reigns. Furthermore, the ancient serpent is bound with a chain and cast into the bottomless pit, because kept away from the hearts of the good and trapped within the minds of the reprobate, he exercises dominion over them with greater savagery. And a little afterwards he is described as being brought out of the depths of the bottomless pit, because from the hearts of the wicked, which now rage secretly, once he has gained power against the Church at that time,[75] he will openly sally forth in the violence of persecution.

From *Moralia* 18.42 [67], 9–22.
CCSL 143A: 932–33.

45. For just as the cedar leaves behind other trees by increasing in height,[76] so too at that time Antichrist, obtaining the glory of the world for a time, surpasses human standards both in the loftiness of his honor and the powerfulness of his signs. For there is a spirit in him who, having been created in the highest regions, did not lose the power of his nature even when he was cast down. So then, at present his power is displayed hardly at all, because he is held bound by the dispensation of divine strength. And so, it is said through John: *I saw an angel coming down from heaven, holding the key of*

75. I.e., at that time when a thousand years are fulfilled and Satan is released from imprisonment.

76. Gregory is commenting on Jb 40.12, *He sets up his tail like a cedar.*

*the bottomless pit and a great chain in his hand. And he seized the dragon, that ancient serpent, who is the Devil and Satan, and bound him for a thousand years, and cast him into the bottomless pit, and shut it, and sealed it over him* (Rv 20.1–3). For he is said to be bound [and cast] into the bottomless pit, because he is thrust into the hearts of the depraved and bound by the power of divine dispensation, to stop him from running unbridled, inflicting harm to the extent that he can. And so as a result, even though he secretly rages through them,[77] he nonetheless does not sally forth in violent spoliations of pride. But in the same passage too it suggests how he will be let loose at the end of the world, when it is said: *And after the thousand years are completed, Satan will be released from his prison, and he will go out and deceive the nations* (Rv 20.7–8). Now because of its perfection the number "thousand" expresses this whole era of the holy Church, however long it may be. When it is completed, the ancient enemy is given back his own powers and let loose against us, for a short time indeed, but with much power.

> From *Moralia* 32.15 [22], 17–39.
> CCSL 143B: 1646–47.

On Revelation 20.6: *Blessed and holy is he who shares in the first resurrection.*

46. *Blessed and holy is he who shares in the first resurrection* (Rv 20.6). For he who afterwards rises again happily in the flesh is the one who, while set in this life, is resurrected from the death of his own mind.

> From *Moralia* 14.16 [19], 7–10.
> CCSL 143A: 708.

On Revelation 20.12: *Books were opened, and another book was opened, which is the book of life. And the dead were judged by what was written in the books.*

47. He who seeks to understand as fully as he can what sort of person he really is must surely look upon those unlike himself, so that from exemplars of good conduct he may measure to what extent he himself has deviated from them by abandoning the good.

---

77. I.e., the depraved.

After all, from those who possess the fullness of the goods,[78] he comes to a correct estimation of what he lacks. And thus in their beauty he beholds his own disgracefulness, which he is able to endure within himself but not to perceive. Now anyone who wants to be a judge of darkness ought to look at light, so that he may see thereby what he should think of the darkness which hinders him from seeing. For if a sinner looks at himself without knowing the conduct of the righteous, he fails to comprehend that he is a sinner. Indeed, he cannot really see himself. For not knowing the brightness of light, when he looks at himself, what does he see other than darkness? So then, we ought to look upon the conduct of the righteous, so that we may gain a precise understanding of our own. For surely what they display is given as a kind of model to be imitated by us. In fact, the conduct of good people is a living book. And so, not unworthily are the same righteous people named "books" in sacred Scripture, as it is written: *Books were opened, and another book was opened, which is the book of life. And the dead were judged by what was written in the books* (Rv 20.12). For the book of life is the very sight of the arriving Judge. Written in it, as it were, is every command, because anyone who casts his eyes upon it soon understands, by the testimony of conscience, whatever he has failed to do. The books are also said to be "opened," because at that time will be manifested the conduct of the righteous, in whom the heavenly commands are seen put into action. "And the dead were judged by what was written in the books," because in the conduct of the righteous, now disclosed, they read as if in an open book the good which they refused to do themselves, and so are condemned by comparison with those who did do it. Therefore, if anyone does not at that time see them and lament what he did not do, let him now study in them what he should imitate.

From *Moralia* 24.8 [15–16], 40–69.
CCSL 143B: 1198–99.

On Revelation 21.1: *There will be a new heaven and a new earth.*
    48. Let us distinguish how earth and heaven either pass away or remain. Both of them pass away in terms of the form which they

---

78. I.e., the virtues.

now possess, but yet continue to exist without end in terms of their essence. And so it is said by Paul: "For the form of this world is passing away."[79] And for this reason Truth himself said: "Heaven and earth will pass away, but my words will not pass away."[80] For this reason too, it is said to John by the voice of the angel: *There will be a new heaven and a new earth* (Rv 21.1). It is not that a different heaven and earth will be created, but the same heaven and earth are renewed. So then, heaven and earth indeed both pass away and will continue to be, because they are cleansed by fire of the form they now possess, and yet they are preserved in their eternal nature. And so, it is said by the psalmist: "You will change them, and they will be changed."[81] This final transformation of theirs they now announce to us by those very alternations which they ceaselessly perform for our benefit. For earth loses its form by the dryness of winter, yet is made green by the moisture of spring. Each day heaven is covered over by the darkness of night and renewed by the brightness of day. Hence, then, hence let every believer realize that both perishing and reestablishment through renewal happen to those things which, it is clear, are constantly restored to life as if from death.

From *Moralia* 17.9 [11], 15–33.
CCSL 143A: 858.

On Revelation 21.12: *It had a great, high wall, with twelve gates, and at the gates twelve angels, and on the gates the names of the twelve tribes of the sons of Israel were inscribed.*

49. The term "gate" can also be understood as every preacher. For anyone whose mouth opens for us a door into the heavenly kingdom is a gate. And so, twelve gates are mentioned both in the Apocalypse of John[82] and in the final vision of this prophet.[83]

From *Homilies on Ezekiel* 2.3 [2],
39–43. CCSL 142: 238.

79. 1 Cor 7.31.
80. Mt 24.35; Mk 13.31; Lk 21.33.
81. Ps 101.27.
82. Cf. Rv 21.12, 21.
83. The prophet Ezekiel; cf. Ezek 40.1–47.

On Revelation 21.17: *A human being's measure, that is, an angel's.*

50. Humility on the part of human beings sometimes brings them to equality with the angels. Thus it is written: "They neither marry nor are given in marriage, but they will be like the angels of God in heaven."[84] And likewise it is said by John: *A human being's measure, that is, an angel's* (Rv 21.17). For a human being is brought unto that height of glory in which the angels rejoice that they are established.

From *Homilies on Ezekiel* 2.2 [15],
398–403. CCSL 142: 236.

On Revelation 21.18: *And the structure of the wall was of jasper, while the city was pure gold, clear as glass.*

51. Now we know the metal gold shines with a brightness superior to all the metals. But the nature of glass is such that what is inside is visible outside with perfect transparency. In the case of other metals, whatever is contained inside is hidden from view; but in the case of glass, any liquid can be seen outside exactly as it is contained inside. And thus all the liquid enclosed in a glass vessel is in plain sight. So then, what else do we understand by gold or glass, if not that heavenly country,[85] that society of blessed citizens, whose hearts mutually shine with brightness upon each other and are mutually transparent to each other by purity? In the Apocalypse John gazed upon this heavenly society, when he said: *And the structure of the wall was of jasper, while the city was pure gold, clear as glass* (Rv 21.18). For since all the saints will shine with the utmost brightness of blessedness, this city is described as built of gold. And since the very brightness of each saint is mutually manifested to the others in their hearts, and since, as soon as the countenance of each is observed, his conscience is also penetrated, it is mentioned that this very gold is like pure glass. For there the corporeity of bodily members will not hide each one's mind from the other's eyes, but rather the soul will be manifested; even the very harmony of the body[86] will be manifested

84. Mt 22.30.
85. Cf. Heb 11.16.
86. One of Aristotle's teachings about the soul suggested that it was a harmony of the body's parts, an idea that was often repeated throughout antiquity.

to corporeal eyes. And thus each at that time will be as transparent to the other as now each is unable to be transparent to himself.

From *Moralia* 18.48 [77–78], 8–30.
CCSL 143A: 941.

On Revelation 22.16: *The bright morning star.*

52. "But when the fullness of time came, God sent his Son born of a woman, made under the law, to redeem those who were under the law."[87] He who was born of a virgin appeared like the morning star[88] amid the darkness of our night, because having put to flight the shadow of sin he proclaimed to us the eternal morning. He made himself known as the morning star,[89] because at daybreak he rose from death and by the brightness of his own light overcame the horrible gloom of our mortality. By John he is rightly called *the bright morning star* (Rv 22.16).[90] For by appearing alive after death he became our morning star,[91] because in providing for us in his own person an exemplar of resurrection, he indicated what light was to follow.

From *Moralia* 29.32 [75], 4–14.
CCSL 143B: 1487.

On Revelation 22.17: *Let him who hears say: Come!*

53. Whoever makes progress by beholding spiritual realities must also offer them to others by recounting them. For he who beholds in order to proclaim is the one who, inasmuch as he makes progress in himself, also preaches out of concern for the progress of his neighbor. For this reason it is written somewhere else: *Let him who hears say: Come!* (Rv 22.17). For when he has already heard the voice of God speaking in his heart, he must unsilence his own voice on behalf of his neighbors through the office of preaching, and thereby call another because he himself has already been called.

From *Homilies on Ezekiel* 2.2 [4],
87–93. CCSL 142: 227.

87. Gal 4.4-5.
88. Lat. *lucifer.*
89. Lat. *lucifer.*
90. Lat. *stella splendida et matutina.*
91. Lat. *matutina stella.*

54. Bring along others as far as you have progressed; desire to have companions on the way to God. If anyone of you, brothers, goes to the marketplace, or perhaps to the public baths, he invites someone whom he sees not otherwise engaged to come with him. This earthly behavior of yours is suitable for you. And if you are going to God, take care not to come to him alone. Thus it is written: *Let him who hears say*: *Come*! (Rv 22.17), so that he who has already received a word of heavenly love in his heart may also impart to his neighbors an external word of exhortation.

> From *Homilies on the Gospels* 6 [6],
> 125–132. CCSL 141: 43.

55. John admonishes through the voice of the angel, when he says: *Let him who hears say*: *Come!* (Rv 22.17). Let the one in whom the inner voice has lodged itself proclaim what he has heard to attract others also to the place where he himself is carried away, lest, even though he was called, he find the doors shut, if he comes without companions near the one who called him.

> From *Book on Pastoral Care* 3.25,
> 47–51. SC 382: 430.

# ANONYMOUS
# GREEK SCHOLIA
# ON THE APOCALYPSE

*Translated by*

T. C. SCHMIDT

# INTRODUCTION

## *ANONYMOUS GREEK SCHOLIA ON THE APOCALYPSE*

In 1911 a Greek manuscript was found in the Meteora monasteries in northern Greece containing chapters 1–14 of the Apocalypse (the Book of Revelation) interspersed with thirty-nine anonymous exegetical notes—or, as scholars have termed them, "scholia."[1] Such a discovery made for an exciting find due to the great rarity of Greek works on the Apocalypse.[2] Together the *Scholia* were of approximately five thousand words in length, and many of them appeared to be highly influenced by Origen of Alexandria with two certainly extracted from the work of Irenaeus of Lyons. As scholars would discover, however, Didymus the Blind and Clement

---

1. For a discussion on this, see Constantin Diobouniotis and Adolf Harnack, "Der Scholien-Kommentar des Origenes zur Apokalypse Johannis nebst einem Stück aus Irenaeus, lib. V, Graece entdeckt und herausgegeben," *Texte und Untersuchungen* 38:3 (1911): 1–3. Scholars have somewhat misleadingly labeled these notes as "scholia" even though they are not marginal notes but are embedded within the main text. For the sake of continuity, however, I use the term.

2. There are only four Greek commentaries extant on the Apocalypse, written by Oecumenius (c. 550 CE), Andrew of Caesarea (c. 600 CE), Arethas of Caesarea (c. 930 CE), and Neophytus the Recluse (1204–1214 CE). For an overview of these writers, see Francis X. Gumerlock, "Patristic Commentaries on Revelation: An Update," *Kerux* 27:3 (2012): 37–43; T. C. Schmidt, *The Book of Revelation and Its Eastern Commentators: Making the New Testament in the Early Christian World* (Cambridge, UK: Cambridge University Press, 2021). For discussion on Neophytus, see Stephen Shoemaker, "The Afterlife of the Apocalypse of John in Byzantine Apocalyptic Literature and Commentary," in *The New Testament in Byzantium*, ed. Derek Krueger and Robert Nelson, 306–13 (Washington, DC: Dumbarton Oaks, 2016); Benedict Englezakis, "An Unpublished Commentary by St Neophytos the Recluse on the Apocalypse," in *Studies on the History of the Church of Cyprus, 4th–20th Centuries*, ed. Misael Ioannou and Silouan Ioannou, 105–46 (Brookfield, VT: Variorum, 1995).

of Alexandria came to be associated with the *Scholia* as well. This introduction to the translation of the *Scholia* briefly describes the manuscript in which they are contained, and then discusses their exegetical method, date, authorship, and sources.

*The Manuscript.* The *Scholia* are preserved in codex Metamorphosis 573, which dates from the 9th or 10th century and is made up of 290 folios.[3] Folios 1r–245r contain various patristic works from writers like Hippolytus, Cyril of Alexandria, and possibly John Cassian, as well as a complete copy of the Apocalypse.[4] The remainder of the manuscript, the part that concerns the present translation,

3. For discussion on the dating of the codex, see Dioubouniotis and Harnack, "Der Scholien-Kommentar," 1; H. C. Hoskier, *Concerning the Text of the Apocalypse* (London: B. Quaritch, Ltd., 1929), 1.653, https://catalog.hathitrust.org/Record/001411390; Panayiotis Tzamalikos, *An Ancient Commentary on the Book of Revelation: A Critical Edition of the Scholia in Apocalypsin* (Cambridge: Cambridge University Press, 2013), 2. The *Kurzgefasste Liste* gives the date as the tenth century; see Institut für Neutestamentliche Textforschung, "Kurzgefasste Liste," New Testament Virtual Manuscript Room, January 16, 2018, http://ntvmr.uni-muenster.de/liste. For an overview of the contents of the codex, see Dioubouniotis and Nikos Athanasios Bées, "Hippolyts Schrift über die Segnungen Jakobs," *Texte und Untersuchungen* 38:1 (1911): 5–9; Tzamalikos, *An Ancient Commentary*, 7–8; Garrick Allen, "The Reception of Scripture and Exegetical Resources in the Scholia in Apocalypsin (GA 2351)," in *Commentaries, Catenae and Biblical Tradition*, ed. H. A. G. Houghton, 141–64 esp. 145 (Piscataway, NJ: Gorgias, 2016); Darius Müller and Edmund Gerke, "Eine deutsche Übersetzung der Scholia in Apocalypsin mit Einleitung," in *Studien zum Text der Apokalypse II*, ed. Marcus Sigismund and Darius Müller, 477–520 esp. 478, Arbeiten zur neutestamentlichen Textforschung 50 (Berlin: De Gruyter, 2017), https://doi.org/10.1515/9783110558784.

4. For a transcription and translation of the works by Cassian, see Panayiotis Tzamalikos, *A Newly Discovered Greek Father: Cassian the Sabaite Eclipsed by John Cassian of Marseilles* (Leiden: Brill, 2012). Tzamalikos denies that these belong to John Cassian, which seems to be why Müller and Allen have listed the author as anonymous or unknown in their own catalogs of the manuscript's contents. For a transcription of one of the works of Hippolytus found in the manuscript, see Dioubouniotis and Bées, "Hippolyts Schrift"; Maurice Brière, Louis Mariès, and B.-Ch. Mercier, eds., *Hippolyte de Rome sur les bénédictions d'Isaac, de Jacob et de Moïse*, Patrologia Orientalis, 27.1–2 (Paris: Firmin-Didot, 1957). The Gregory-Aland number for this copy of the Apocalypse is 2329, not 2321 as Hoskier claimed; see J. K. Elliott, "Manuscripts of the Book of Revelation Collated by H. C. Hoskier," *The Journal of Theological Studies* 40:1 (1989): 100–111, 104, https://doi.org/10.1093/jts/40.1.100; Hoskier, *Concerning the Text of the Apocalypse*, 2.19. Hoskier designates the manuscript as number 200 according to his catalog.

contains another copy of the Apocalypse up to chapter 14, verse 5, with thirty-nine scholia inserted at various intervals.[5]

*Exegetical Method.* Though coming from multiple sources, most of the scholia seem to stem from the same theological milieu. Other than Scholia 38 and 39, which are excerpted in part from Irenaeus, the *Scholia* consistently attempt to look past a "physical" or literal interpretation of the Apocalypse in an effort to attain to a "spiritual" or mystical reading of the text. For example, Scholion 14 says, "But since the Word concerns spiritual things, one must proceed higher, beyond any physical manifestation concerning [this] stone. Therefore, on the spiritual *stone*, [which is] white on account of [its] radiance, a *new name is written* according to the New Covenant, which symbolizes the quality of the one who received it and knows it."[6]

In conjunction with this approach, the historical background of the Apocalypse is completely ignored but for three brief exceptions. The first is Scholion 13, which instructs the reader to "refer the historical events [in this passage] to the deceivers evidenced here," but does not dwell on the matter further. The only other historical discussions take place in Scholia 31 and 32, both of which merely refer to the historical background of the Apocalypse in order to demonstrate that "a physical interpretation brings a great impossibility,"[7] which then allows the author to offer a spiritual interpretation.

Additionally, the *Scholia* do not attempt to venture into historical or eschatological discussion even when the text of the Apocalypse

5. The Gregory-Aland number is 2351, not 2322 as Hoskier states in his table of manuscripts; see Elliott, "Manuscripts of the Book of Revelation Collated by H. C. Hoskier," 104; Hoskier, *Concerning the Text of the Apocalypse*, 2.19. Hoskier designates the manuscript as number 201 according to his catalog. A fragment of this particular manuscript may also be found in the national Library of Russia, MS gr. 383; see Nadezhda Kavrus-Hoffmann, "Catalogue of Greek Medieval and Renaissance Manuscripts in the Collections of the United States of America, Part V.1: Harvard University, The Houghton Library," *Manuscripta* 54:1 (2010): 105, https://doi.org/10.1484/J.MSS.1.100788.

6. See, for example, Scholia 7 and 27, which instruct the reader to look beyond the physical or literal interpretation; also Scholia 9, 19, and 28, where the Scholia attend to the spiritual meaning of the text.

7. Scholion 31.

seems to invite such an avenue of interpretation. For example, in
Scholia 29–33, which cover the opening of the seven seals in Apocalypse chapters 5–7, no mention is made that the events may refer
to a future (or past) time. On the other hand, Scholion 37 is one
of the few places that seem to mention any kind of eschatological
framework; the author speaks of "the *time* of the consummation,
when all shall appear before the judgment seat of Christ in order
that each shall deservedly receive according to how he has lived."
But after this relatively general pronouncement, the author does
not elaborate upon it and quickly moves on to a discussion concerning the proper interpretation of the titles "*prophets* and *saints* and
others *who fear the name* of God."

The *Scholia* are furthermore concerned with clearing up apparent contradictions in the Apocalypse. Scholion 1 takes great pains
to show how Jesus's statement in Jn 15.15, that his disciples were
friends not slaves, "does not disagree with what was confessed by
them concerning themselves, that they are slaves of the Lord."[8]
Scholion 25 even goes so far as to construct an interpretation that
does "not incur derision from the wise of the world" even though a
literal interpretation would not be contradictory.[9]

The *Scholia* also show considerable interest in the interpretation
of individual words of Scripture. Scholion 29 discusses the difference between "people" and "nation," while Scholion 11 discusses
the different meanings of "first death" and "second death." This
emphasis on nomenclature occurs frequently throughout the *Scholia.*[10]

Lastly, the style of the *Scholia* can be quite desultory at times,
jumping from subject to subject with occasionally a thin reason for
doing so. Scholion 30 is the chief example of this; it begins with a
somewhat unrelated discussion about the nature of God's physical
faculties and then moves on to a digression on the nature of God's
wrath and finally concludes with some theological musings about
the nature of angels. Most of the *Scholia*, however, do not engage
in such severe digressions, but move from topic to topic by relating
a phrase or word in the Apocalypse to another part of Scripture.

8. See Scholia 10 and 11 for further examples.
9. See also Scholion 6.
10. See Scholia 1, 2, 3, 4, 9, and 37 for further examples.

For example, Scholion 6, which comments on the "double-edged sword" in Rv 1.16, cites a similar passage in Ps 56, then moves on to a passage in Matthew, and finally concludes by alluding to a passage in the Song of Songs.[11]

All these tendencies are hallmarks of the exegetical tradition typically associated with writers of the "Alexandrian" interpretive milieu, as scholars have pointed out before.[12] In fact, aside from Scholia 38 and 39, the content of which is derived mostly from Irenaeus, it is rare to find exegesis that is not indicative of Alexandrian exegesis.

*Date.* The *Scholia* do not discuss any historical or contemporary details that might give specific footholds for dating. Scholia 7, 22, and 26 may contain Christological discussions that correspond with fourth-century Christological concerns,[13] but this is not certain, given that such language could conceivably come from earlier or later times as well. Scholia 4 and 7 call John the "Theologian" (Θεολόγος), a term that did not gain currency until the fourth or fifth century, but the word could simply be an interpolation from a later scholiast.[14] Additionally, Scholion 25 is concerned with how non-Christians might interpret Scripture, which may fit best within an ante-Nicene context, but this observation must be tempered by the fact that we do find writers in the sixth century worrying over how non-Christian sensibilities might clash with the Apocalypse.[15]

Most relevant for dating purposes, however, is that the *Scholia* do not exhibit the theological concerns of the fifth through eighth centuries, such as anti-Origenism, monophysitism, iconoclasm, mono-

11. See, for example, Scholia 9 and 12.

12. A. de Boysson, "Avons-nous un commentaire d'Origène sur l'Apocalypse?" *Revue Biblique (1892–1940)* 10:4 (1913): 537; Tzamalikos, *An Ancient Commentary*, xiii. For a discussion problematizing the classification of "Alexandrian" and "Antiochene" exegesis, see Frances M. Young, *Biblical Exegesis and the Formation of Christian Culture* (Cambridge and New York: Cambridge University Press, 1997), 209–12, http://site.ebrary.com/id/10450680.

13. For example, Scholion 7 insists that Jesus is the first "not in time, but in honor," Scholion 22 cautions that Jesus should not be called a κτίσμα, and Scholion 26 argues that the existence of Jesus is not dependent on the will of the Father.

14. See discussion and footnotes to Scholion 4.

15. For example, Oecumenius, *Commentary on the Apocalypse* 10.11 (FC 112: 160–62).

thelitism, nor even the rise of Islam. This points to an origin of the *Scholia* in the second through fourth centuries.

*Authorship and Sources.* The lack of hard evidence concerning the sources of many of the *Scholia* has not dissuaded scholars from attempting to identify their authors. Adolf Harnack was the first to mount an effort in this regard and theorized on the basis of theological and stylistic parallels that Scholia 1–37 and the first part of 38 came from Origen.[16] In further support of this idea, Harnack noted how Origen also stated that he had written or intended to write a work on the Apocalypse in his *Commentary on Matthew* 49: "It is not the time to explain separately all these things concerning the seven heads of the Dragon.... But this will be explained in its own time on the Apocalypse of John ... but the principal expositions and examinations of these things ought to occur when the book itself will have been presented to us for explanation. Now, however, it is necessary to explain this only ..."[17] But from this remark alone, it is not entirely clear that Origen did compose a work devoted to the Apocalypse. Shortly afterwards, for example, Origen provided some exegesis of the Apocalypse, so it is possible that the Latin translator misconstrued some of Origen's remarks and that Origen therefore was merely referring to some comments he would shortly make, and not to a dedicated commentary or homiletical series. Another possibility is that Origen was only hypothetically mentioning that further exegetical insight into the Apocalypse must wait for a more opportune time, if one should ever arise. On the other

16. Diobouniotis and Harnack, "Der Scholien-Kommentar," 45–66.

17. My translation from *Origenes Werke: Commentarius in Matthaeum*, Die Griechischen Christlichen Schriftsteller, 38.2 (Leipzig: J. C. Hinrichs, 1899), comm. ser. 49, page 105, lines 5–17, http://archive.org/details/origeneswerkehrs11origuoft. In Origen's *Homilies on Ezekiel* 6.4.2 he may also refer to a commentary on the Apocalypse, though most likely he is referring to a commentary on the book of Job: "It is written in Job about the Dragon: 'His power is in his navel, and his strength is in the navel of his belly.' I know from the things that divine grace granted to me that when I explained the current passage, I said that the Dragon represents contrary strength. For he is 'the Dragon, the ancient serpent, who is called the devil and Satan, deceiving the whole world' [Apocalypse 12:4]." Translation by Thomas P. Scheck, *Origen: Homilies 1–14 on Ezekiel*, ACW 62 (New York: Paulist Press, 2010), 90.

hand, there is a pseudo-Isidorian preface from the late sixth century, attached to a ninth-century manuscript of the Hiberno-Latin *Handbook on the Apocalypse of the Apostle John*, which claims to know of twelve homilies by Origen on the Apocalypse,[18] suggesting that Origen did comment on the book. In balance, then, it is possible that Origen did write some kind of work on the Apocalypse, but this cannot be known with certainty without more evidence.

Harnack at least acknowledged, however, that the second part of Scholion 38 and all of 39 were derived from Irenaeus's *Against Heresies*. Along with this analysis, Harnack furnished the *editio princeps* of the *Scholia* with, as Armitage Robinson put it, "characteristic speed";[19] it was published only six months after he first received a copy of the manuscript. The publication of the text generated much interest and criticism, but the haste in which it was produced came at the price of accuracy. Herman C. Hoskier, for example, stated that Harnack's edition contained "innumerable errors" and scolded Harnack for his negligence.[20]

Within a year of publication several scholars had written articles proposing improvements upon the Greek text or had set forth further thoughts on the author or authors of the *Scholia*.[21] Shortly

18. Joseph F. T. Kelly, "Early Medieval Evidence for Twelve Homilies by Origen on the Apocalypse," *Vigiliae Christianae* 39:3 (1985): 273–79, esp. 273–74, https://doi.org/10.2307/1583857.

19. J. Armitage Robinson, "Origen's Comments on the Apocalypse," *The Journal of Theological Studies* 13, no. 50 (1912): 295–97, 295.

20. Hoskier, *Concerning the Text of the Apocalypse*, 1.657. Turner, though noting several errors, was less critical; C. H. Turner, "The Text of the Newly Discovered Scholia of Origen on the Apocalypse," *The Journal of Theological Studies* 13, no. 51 (1912): 386–97, 386, https://doi.org/10.1093/jts/os-XIII.51.386.

21. Robinson, "Origen's Comments on the Apocalypse"; Gustav Wohlenberg, "Ein neuaufgefundener Kodex der Offenbarung Johannis nebst alten Erläuterungen," *Theologisches Literaturblatt* 33:2 (1912): cols. 25–30; Gustav Wohlenberg, "Ein neuaufgefundener Kodex der Offenbarung Johannis nebst alten Erläuterungen" (part 2), *Theologisches Literaturblatt* 33:3 (1912): cols. 49–57; Gustav Wohlenberg, "Noch einiges zu dem Scholienkommentar (des Origenes) zur Offenbarung Johannis," *Theologisches Literaturblatt* 33:10 (1912): cols. 217–20; Otto Stählin, "Der Scholien-Kommentar des Origenes zur Apokalypse Johannis," *Berliner philologische wochenschrift* 32:5 (1912): 132–40; Erich Klostermann, "Der Scholien-Kommentar des Origenes zur Apokalypse Johannis," *Theologische Literaturzeitung* 27:3 (1912): 73–74; Franz Diekamp, "Diobouniotis, Constantin, und Adolf Harnack, Der Scholien-Kommentar des Origenes zur Apokalypse Johannis," *Theologische Revue* 11:2 (1912):

afterwards C. H. Turner and Hoskier made great efforts at correcting Harnack's text while others continued to discuss the authorship of the *Scholia*.[22] These scholars chipped away at Harnack's theory that Origen was responsible for Scholia 1–38a, and many of their observations are pertinent for the present consideration of the same issue.

Gustav Wohlenberg, for instance, argued that any single scholion may actually contain quotations from multiple authors because Scholion 38 begins with a paragraph from an anonymous author and then, completely unannounced, supplies a fragment from Irenaeus.[23] Wohlenberg further pointed out that many authors after Origen made use of his works, and provided examples from Jerome and his *Commentary on Ephesians*.[24] This, therefore, would make it very difficult to attribute definitively any of the *Scholia* to Origen simply on the basis of shared thought.[25]

But perhaps the most devastating blow came from T. Schermann and Otto Stählin, who each independently pointed out that Scholion 5 was a direct excerpt from Clement of Alexandria's *Stromateis*.[26] This showed decisively that the *Scholia* were excerpted from multiple authors. Schermann and Stählin also demonstrated that the *Scholia* may not have been taken from a commentary specifically on the Apocalypse, as the three scholia that had been identified (5, 38b, and 39) were from patristic works that only mentioned the

51–55; Theod. Schermann, "Ein Scholienkommentar des Origenes?" *Theologische Revue* 11:1 (1912): 29.

22. Turner, "The Text of the Newly Discovered Scholia of Origen on the Apocalypse"; C. H. Turner, "Origen Scholia in Apocalypsin," *The Journal of Theological Studies* 25, no. 97 (1923): 1–16, https://doi.org/10.1093/jts/os-XXV.97.1; Hoskier, *Concerning the Text of the Apocalypse*. Turner and Hoskier do not seem to have been aware of each other's work. Other scholars to discuss the *Scholia* include de Boysson, "Avons-nous un commentaire d'Origène sur l'Apocalypse?"; Eiliv Skard, "Zum Scholien-kommentar des Origenes zur Apokalypse Johannis," *Symbolae Osloenses* 15:1 (1936): 204–8; Pierre Nautin, *Origène: Sa vie et son œuvre* (Paris: Beauchesne, 1977), 449.

23. Wohlenberg, "Ein neuaufgefundener Kodex der Offenbarung Johannis nebst alten Erläuterungen" (part 2), col. 50.

24. Wohlenberg, col. 52.

25. Wohlenberg, cols. 52–53.

26. Schermann, "Ein Scholienkommentar des Origenes?" 29; Stählin, "Der Scholien-Kommentar," 135.

Apocalypse incidentally. A. de Boysson and Stählin also attempted to find further parallels with Clement of Alexandria, but both admitted that parallels with Origen were far more persuasive, except of course in the case of Scholion 5.[27]

We owe the next phase of authorship studies to the 1941 discovery of various works by Didymus the Blind, including especially his *Commentary on Zechariah*, where he may indicate that he had written a work on the Apocalypse.[28] When discussing the 144,000 virgins of Rv 14.3–4, he says, "... it is a squared number, with the combined factors of twelve expressed in thousands, twelve being a much-used figure, as it is clear to one browsing through the Scriptures. An irrefutable explanation of this has been given in the works on the Apocalypse of John ..."[29] It was not, however, until the 1980s that Eric Junod suggested that Didymus may lie behind portions of the *Scholia*, though he did not investigate this possibility in depth.[30]

In the same decade a French translation of the *Scholia* was made by Solange Bouquet, and in the brief, two-page introduction by Adalbert-Gautier Hamman, Harnack's theory is dismissed.[31]

27. Stählin, "Der Scholien-Kommentar," 140; de Boysson, "Avons-nous un commentaire d'Origène sur l'Apocalypse?" 559.

28. For discussions about this manuscript discovery see Louis Doutreleau, ed., *Didyme l'Aveugle: Sur Zacharie*, SC 83–85 (vol. 1–3) (Paris: Cerf, 1962), 1.21–23; Pierre Nautin, ed., *Didyme l'Aveugle: Sur la Genèse*, SC 233, 244 (vol.1–2) (Paris: Cerf, 1977), 1.11–19.

29. Translation from Robert C. Hill, trans., Didymus the Blind, *Commentary On Zechariah*, FC 111 (Washington, DC: The Catholic University of America Press, 2013), 201. The original Greek is located in *Commentary on Zechariah* 3.73 of Doutreleau, *Didyme l'Aveugle: Sur Zacharie*.

30. Eric Junod, "À propos des soi-disant scolies sur l'Apocalypse d'Origène," *Rivista di storia e letteratura religiosa* 20 (1984): 112–21 esp. 119–21. Wohlenberg also had suggested links with Didymus; Wohlenberg, "Ein neuaufgefundener Kodex der Offenbarung Johannis nebst alten Erläuterungen" (part 2), cols. 53, 55–56, and footnotes.

31. Joël Courreau and Adalbert-Gautier Hamman, eds., *L'Apocalypse expliquée par Césaire d'Arles. Scholies attribuées à Origène*, trans. Solange Bouquet (Paris: Desclée de Brouwer, 1989), 164–65. Ilaria Ramelli has also briefly mentioned the authorship of the *Scholia* and believes that some of them stem from Origen. She also mentions a work in Polish on the authorship of the *Scholia*, which I am not able to consult. See Ilaria L. E. Ramelli, "Origen's Anti-Subordinationism and its Heritage in the Nicene and Cappadocian Line," *Vigiliae Christianae* 65:1 (2011): 46 note 2.

More recently Garrick Allen has discussed the exegetical techniques found in the *Scholia* as well as the physical features of their
manuscript. Darius Müller and Edmund Gerke have also furnished
a German translation with a brief introduction.[32] Allen, Müller,
and Gerke have all rightly maintained that the *Scholia* stem from
multiple authors.[33]

The largest contribution in this recent stage of studies has, however, come from Panayiotis Tzamalikos, who has written an entire
book devoted to the *Scholia*.[34] Tzamalikos very helpfully provides a
new edition of the Greek text and an English translation, but his
book is marred by poor organization, a tendency to make unneces-
sary conjectural emendations,[35] and a neglect to indicate where his
text differs from Harnack, Turner, or Hoskier.[36] A further defect is
his constant insistence that the *Scholia* were produced by a certain
sixth-century Cassian the Sabaite, who, Tzamalikos argues, occasionally quoted from writers like Clement of Alexandria, Irenaeus,
Didymus, and Origen when composing the *Scholia*.

Now the particular Cassian that Tzamalikos has in mind is not
the fifth-century John Cassian of monastic fame, but a hitherto unknown figure who, he says, was perhaps "the last great scholar of
Eastern Christianity."[37] Tzamalikos attributes the *Scholia* to him
because on folio 1r of the *Scholia*'s manuscript there are two headings that read, "The book of Cassian the Monk," and, "By Monk
Cassian the Roman."[38] Another similar statement can be found on
the last folio of the manuscript (and of the *Scholia*), which reads, "By
Monk Cassian the Roman."[39] Tzamalikos knows that this cannot refer to the manuscript's principal scribe, Theodosius, because

32. Müller and Gerke, "Eine deutsche Übersetzung."
33. Müller and Gerke, 435–37; Allen, "The Reception of Scripture and Exegetical Resources in the Scholia in Apocalypsin (GA 2351)," 146–47.
34. Tzamalikos, *An Ancient Commentary*.
35. See, for example, at Scholion 26.
36. Tzamalikos, *An Ancient Commentary*, 87.
37. Tzamalikos, 94.
38. Tzamalikos, 7.
39. Tzamalikos, 76. Tzamalikos gives this folio as 295r, but in another volume
he gives the correct location (along with a picture), which is folio 290r; Panayiotis
Tzamalikos, *The Real Cassian Revisited: Monastic Life, Greek Paideia, and Origenism in
the Sixth Century* (Leiden: Brill, 2012), 548.

he left us his own colophon.[40] So instead, Tzamalikos posits both that Cassian was responsible for having the content of the book transcribed and that he was the author of the content as well.[41] He insists on this despite the fact that, as he admits, the ninth- or tenth-century codex cannot have belonged to a sixth-century author (Tzamalikos says that the codex is a copy of the supposed original, but gives no evidence for this)[42] and that Tzamalikos's Cassian is from the Eastern Empire and therefore not of Latin origin, as the moniker "Cassian the Roman" implies.[43]

Furthermore, the final statement attributing the codex to Cassian may not indicate authorship at all, for it is written by a later hand—a fact that suggests the work of a Renaissance cataloguer who noticed that the codex began with works by John Cassian and hastily (and incorrectly) scribbled the attribution at the conclusion of the manuscript. Such attributions may also be markers of ownership written by someone who later possessed the codex, as Tzamalikos acknowledges.[44] Such possibilities seem all the more reasonable because there are other works in the codex that are definitely not by Cassian, such as writings of Cyril of Alexandria and Hippolytus as well as a complete copy of the Apocalypse.[45] Several of Tzamalikos's reviewers have made similar points and have criticized him for being overly speculative.[46]

40. For descriptions of the colophon of Theodosius, see Tzamalikos, *An Ancient Commentary*, 2–3, 8; Hoskier, *Concerning the Text of the Apocalypse*, 1.637–38.

41. These assertions are scattered throughout his volume; see, for example, Tzamalikos, *An Ancient Commentary*, 9, 60, 63, 66, 91–92.

42. Tzamalikos, 76.

43. Tzamalikos, *The Real Cassian*, 230. This was also noted by Kellen Plaxco, "An Ancient Commentary on the Book of Revelation: A Critical Edition of the Scholia in Apocalypsin. Translated and Edited by Panagiotes Tzamalikos," *Theological Studies* 75:4 (2014): 905, https://doi.org/10.1177/0040563914548658c. It is of course possible that Cassian could have been from "New Rome" (i.e., Constantinople), but this does not seem as likely.

44. Tzamalikos, *An Ancient Commentary*, 74.

45. Tzamalikos argues that the headings must refer to the person responsible for the contents of the entire codex, and not merely to the earlier works in the codex (which the manuscript attributes to a Cassian) because otherwise the repeated headings would contain redundant information; Tzamalikos, 76. Yet manuscripts often redundantly repeat information, and, as I pointed out above, clearly there are works in this codex that do not belong to Tzamalikos's Cassian.

46. Reviews and articles that discuss Tzamalikos include Garrick Allen, "Review

Thus, the two major attempts at identifying a single author of the *Scholia* have not been successful. Harnack's theory that the *Scholia* stem from a work of Origen was viewed as overreaching by scholars of his day, and Tzamalikos's attempts to attribute them to an unknown Cassian seem just as unconvincing. Clearly the scholiast has used excerpts from multiple authors because we find verbatim excerpts from works by Clement of Alexandria and Irenaeus.

There is, however, reason to believe that Origen and Didymus the Blind may also lurk behind many of the unidentified scholia. Not only do Origen and Didymus match the exegetical profile of the *Scholia* in that they are both of the Alexandrian tradition, but it is certain that both treated the Apocalypse at length in their writings, even if they did not write works specifically on the text (though they both may have). Additionally, there are many verbal parallels that can be drawn between the *Scholia* and these two writers, the most salient of which are indicated at appropriate points in the footnotes of the present translation. For example, Scholia 3, 11, 17, 28, and 30 employ wording that is used by no other ancient Christian author except Origen, as with the phrases ἀπολυθήσεται τοῦ περισπασμοῦ, "doubts will be solved," and οὐ φύσεως ἀπολλυμένης, "not of the nature of destruction." Likewise,

---

of an Ancient Commentary on the Book of Revelation: A Critical Edition of the Scholia in Apocalypsin by P. Tzamalikos," *The Two Cities* (blog), October 4, 2014, http://www.thetwocities.com/book-reviews/review-of-an-ancient-commentary -on-the-book-of-revelation-a-critical-edition-of-the-scholia-in-apocalypsin-by- p-tzamalikos/; Allen, "The Reception of Scripture and Exegetical Resources in the Scholia in Apocalypsin (GA 2351)," 146; Jean-Marie Auwers, "An Ancient Commentary on the Book of Revelation: A Critical Edition of the Scholia in Apocalypsin," *Ephemerides Theologicae Lovanienses* 90:4 (2014): 781; D. C. Parker, "An Ancient Commentary on the Book of Revelation. A Critical Edition of the 'Scholia in Apocalypsin' by P. Tzamalikos," *The Journal of Ecclesiastical History* 66:2 (2015): 391–93, https:// doi.org/10.1017/S0022046914002723; Plaxco, "An Ancient Commentary"; Müller and Gerke, "Eine deutsche Übersetzung," 485–87. No reviewer was convinced by Tzamalikos's argument that an unknown Cassian was responsible for the *Scholia*. Plaxco, for example, said that Tzamalikos's theory "is at worst unconvincing and at best a tenuous and speculative assertion that begs for cogently articulated support"; Plaxco, "An Ancient Commentary," 905. Auwers is the only reviewer I could find who does not criticize Tzamalikos for the nature of his arguments, but even he does not openly embrace them; instead, Auwers says that he is convinced that Didymus was behind many of the scholia.

Scholia 1, 18, 26, and 31 have wording that is used by no other ancient Christian author except Didymus when they deploy terms like
ἐλαττωτικός, "not insisting on full rights," and δυνάμενοι φάναι,
"who are able to say." In a similar vein, Scholia 4, 6, 12, 15, 20, 27,
29, 30, 32, and 36 express thoughts and arguments quite similar
to those found in the works of Origen, while Scholia 9, 10, 13, 21,
22, 28, and 31 parallel Didymus's writings. These links with Origen and Didymus, however, must be tempered with statements that
seem to conflict with what we know of one or both authors, as is the
case with Scholion 7. There are also other instances when a strong
parallel can be found in a non-Christian author, as with Scholion
33, showing that a parallel may not necessarily be indicative of authorship. And there are times when certain scholia provide parallels with both Origen and Didymus, as with Scholia 13, 17, 19,
28, and 36, suggesting that perhaps it is vain to search for a single
author of every scholion.

With this in mind, it is important to note that one can draw further links between certain groups of scholia and Origen by using
the following method. First, many of the scholia appear related to
one another because of their similarity of wording and theological
concern (Scholia 6 and 12; 15 and 30; 20 and 27). Secondly, several scholia appear related to one another because they parallel
the same passage in a work of Origen. These connections make it
possible to build a multi-layered web of relationships between some
scholia and Origen by linking various groups of scholia together
through primary, secondary, and tertiary connections. Thus Scholia 15 and 30 parallel one another in regard to their content, but
both are further connected because they parallel Origen's *Homilies on Genesis* 1.13, the very same passage that is also paralleled by
Scholion 36. But Scholion 30 also parallels *Homilies on Luke* 13.5–6,
which in turn is paralleled by Scholia 6 and 12, both of which are
directly related to one another. It is therefore possible to chart a
network of relationships among Scholia 6, 12, 15, 30, and 36, all of
which ultimately lead back to Origen.[47] Similar relationships can
be charted between Didymus and Scholia 21 and 22.

47. Likewise, Scholia 20 and 27 parallel one another in content, but are also
further connected to each other in that they parallel the same passage in Origen's
*Homilies on Exodus* 12.4.

Such verbal and theological parallels do seem to highlight the role that Origen and Didymus played in either writing or inspiring many of the scholia. Additional support for this idea can be found in two scholia that contain indications that they were excerpted from larger works that concerned the Apocalypse specifically,[48] perhaps the very kind of works that Origen and Didymus seem to have written. Yet, despite the correspondences with these two writers, I have refrained from identifying them as the authors of any of the scholia without more explicit evidence. As Wohlenberg pointed out above, who can tell if these parallels exist because an author was working in the same intellectual milieu as Origen and Didymus, or if a later editor was re-composing excerpts from the two writers? This latter scenario was commonplace. Methodius of Olympus and Procopius of Gaza cite Origen frequently, but do not preserve his quotations verbatim, though they evidently preserve the sense of his passages.[49] The same can be said for the anonymous excerptor of Origen's *Against Celsus* and the Greek fragments of Origen's *Commentary on Romans*, both of which appear to be summaries, not direct quotations.[50] Additionally, one catenist (or later scribe) who used Origen's *Commentary on John* introduced numerous inaccuracies in his own excerpts of Origen.[51] Some writers also repurposed material from Origen, as Jerome and Eusebius both did when they reused much of Origen's exegesis for their own projects.[52] Something similar to these kinds of repurposing may therefore have occurred in the production of the *Scholia*. One can see, for example, that the scholiast did not precisely preserve his source material because in the quotations of Irenaeus in Scholia 38 and 39 the scholiast inserts a paragraph from an unknown source before

48. Scholia 32 and 36.

49. Henri Crouzel, *Origen* (Edinburgh: T. & T. Clark, 1999), 45.

50. Miroslav Marcovich, ed., *Origenes. Contra Celsum Libri VIII* (Leiden: Brill, 2001), xii; Thomas P. Scheck, trans., Origen, *Commentary on the Epistle to the Romans, Books 1–5*, FC 105 (Washington, DC: The Catholic University of America Press, 2009), 17–18.

51. Ronald E. Heine, trans., Origen, *Commentary on the Gospel According to John: Books 1–10*, FC 80 (Washington, DC: The Catholic University of America Press, 1989), 9–10.

52. Thomas P. Scheck, trans., St. Jerome, *Commentary on Isaiah*; Origen, *Homilies 1–9 on Isaiah*, ACW 68 (New York: Paulist Press, 2015), 25–26, 33–36.

an unannounced quotation of Irenaeus. And even in the material unique to Irenaeus, the scholiast omits content without indicating so.[53]

Further caution against ascribing the unidentified scholia to
Origen or Didymus in a wholesale fashion is due to the fact that
clearly other scholia, Scholia 5, 38b, and 39, come from other authors (Clement of Alexandria and Irenaeus). A similar phenomenon also presents itself with the *Philocalia*, which purports to excerpt various interesting passages from the works of Origen, but
occasionally draws from other writers.[54] This suggests that authors
other than Origen and Didymus may also be present in the unidentified scholia.

But the greatest deterrent to positively identifying authors
emerged with the discovery of Didymus's *Commentary on Zechariah* in the 1940s. If this work had never been found, then parallels
between the *Scholia* and Didymus would never have been noticed,
nor would scholars have known that Didymus may have written a
commentary on the Apocalypse. It follows that future discoveries
could therefore provide definitive evidence that many or all of the
noted parallels between Origen and Didymus could be simply co-
incidental or, alternatively, could stem from the same theological
episteme. Thus our watchword should be caution. Scholars who
use the unidentified scholia should treat them as being authored
by multiple figures who probably flourished in the second through
fourth centuries and who mostly employed Alexandrian exegesis.
Origen and Didymus should be regarded as primary lines of influence on many of the scholia, but their authorship, while often likely,
is ultimately uncertain.

*The Collection of the Scholia.* Though determining when and where
the scholiast lived is difficult, there are several reasons for believing
that he did his work in Egypt in the fifth or the sixth century. To
begin with, the scholiast probably lived after the year 400 (shortly
after Didymus the Blind died in 398 CE, who is likely quoted in the
*Scholia*), but before the tenth century (when the manuscript of the

53. See the omitted paragraph from *Against Heresies* 5.28.2 in Scholion 38.
54. *Philocalia* 23.21–22; 24.1–8; this is not a precise analog, however, because
here the other authors are explicitly made known to the reader.

*Scholia* was copied). It so happens that between 400 and 900 CE,
the Apocalypse had greatly fallen in prestige in the Greek church
and was thus rarely copied and rarely quoted. Greek Egypt is the
only exception to this phenomenon, where the Apocalypse was always treated with favor.[55] This and the fact that most of the prob-
able sources of the *Scholia* are Alexandrian (Clement of Alexandria,
Didymus the Blind, and Origen of Alexandria) suggest a prove-
nance of Egypt. This locale also helps to narrow the timeframe of
the *Scholia*'s collection further—for after the Islamic conquests of
Egypt in the early seventh century, Greek Christianity practical-
ly vanished from Egypt, implying that the scholiast lived before
the mid-seventh century. This timeframe also helps to explain why
Andrew of Caesarea (c. 600 CE) is never excerpted in the *Scholia*,
even though his commentary on the Apocalypse dominated the
Greek reception of Revelation from the seventh century onwards.
Similarly, the scholiast also does not quote from the lesser-known
Oecumenius (c. 550 CE), whose allegorical commentary on the
Apocalypse would have likely been much appreciated by him. For
these reasons, a tentative date for the scholiast's activity seems to be
sometime in the fifth or the sixth century, and the location seems
likely, though not certainly, to be in Egypt. Such a dating also provides sufficient time for the *Scholia* to go through several generations
of copying, allowing for the occasional confused copying of certain
scholia, as can be seen in the remaining manuscript.[56]

*The Translation.* A rough draft of this translation was completed
in 2011 at the request of Frank Gumerlock. At the time, I used the
edition of Harnack while consulting Hoskier and Turner throughout. After Tzamalikos's edition was published in 2013, I revised the
translation, checking it carefully against Tzamalikos's text and ac-
cepting many of his suggested changes to the Greek text. I indicate
in the footnotes whenever I have preferred a reading by Turner and
whenever I reject Tzamalikos's conjectural emendations. I employ
a fairly literal translation method to help highlight the difference
between the style utilized by the text of Revelation and that of the

55. For a thorough description of the reception of the Apocalypse in the Greek
church, see Schmidt, *The Book of Revelation and Its Eastern Commentators*, 159–204.
56. See, for example, Scholia 20 and 21.

*Scholia*. Words in brackets are not explicit in the Greek text, and italicized words indicate that the author is utilizing vocabulary derived from the Apocalypse. For biblical references, I cite only direct quotations or very clear allusions. When the *Scholia* quote from the Apocalypse, I do not provide a citation unless the quotation comes from a section of the Apocalypse not placed immediately before a scholion in the manuscript. Greek word parallels were found by consulting the TLG database in 2011 and were rechecked in August 2018. Any parallels that I first learned from Tzamalikos I note in the footnotes.[57] Though I discovered numerous parallels, I note only the most significant in the footnotes. The most important of those that I do note, I have also placed in the table below for easy reference.

| Scholia | Parallels between the *Scholia* and Ancient Authors |
|---|---|
| 1 | **Didymus** is the only Christian author before the 10th century to make use of the lexeme ἐλαττωτικός ("not insisting on full rights") in any form. As in the *Scholia*, Didymus also uses the lexeme with the genitive reflexive pronoun. |
| | **Origen** similarly explains why the apostles called themselves "slaves" in his *Commentary on Romans* 1.1.1, though he uses different biblical passages in support of the idea. |
| 2 | |
| 3 | **Origen** is the only known writer who uses, closely together, the terms "apostle," "evangelist," and "prophet" in association with the name John (*Commentary on John* 2.45), as this scholion does. |
| 4 | **Origen**, *On Prayer* 27.13, contains a very similar idea involving the term "day" and the threefold nature of time mentioned in Hebrews 13.8, just as this scholion contains, but such sentiments are found in other authors as well; see Tzamalikos, *An Ancient Commentary*, 218–19. Also, the scholion uses the fourth-century term "John the Theologian," which Origen likely did not use. |

57. Whenever I had reason to search only Christian authors in the TLG database, I segmented them out according to the TLG epithet "Scr. Eccl."

| Scholia | **Parallels between the *Scholia* and Ancient Authors** |
|---|---|
| 5 | This scholion is an excerpt from **Clement of Alexandria,** *Stromateis* 4.25.156–157. |
| 6 | **Origen's** *Commentary on John* 1.229 parallels this scholion both in its general content and in that it draws upon the same passages from the Gospel of Matthew, the Epistle to the Hebrews, and the Song of Songs. Other parallels can be found in Origen, *Homilies on the Psalms*, Ps. 36 hom. 3.3 and Ps. 76 hom. 3.5. This scholion also parallels Origen's *Homilies on Luke* 13.4–6, the same passage paralleled by Scholia 12 and 30. This scholion seems further connected with Scholion 12 on the basis of their shared content. Tzamalikos does note other, though less impressive, parallels with authors like **Didymus** and **Theodoret;** see Tzamalikos, *An Ancient Commentary*, 224. |
| 7 | The theology of this scholion appears to come from the fourth century and is perhaps even Arian. It also appears to contradict Origen and contains the fourth-century term "John the Theologian." **Didymus** does, however, vaguely parallel thoughts in this scholion when he discusses the same passage in Revelation in his *Commentary on Ecclesiastes*, 11–12 P. 328; see Tzamalikos, 227. |
| 8 | |
| 9 | **Didymus** in his *Commentarii in Psalmos* 22–26.10, page 107, lines 22–25 (TLG #2102.017), speaks of the idea that the number 7 is holy and blessed. The scholion shares thematic content with Scholion 28. |
| 10 | This scholion uses the Greek word ἀγαπητικός, the lexeme of which is used 7 times by **Didymus**, though not at all by Origen. The lexeme, however, is used by many other Christian authors including **Clement of Alexandria**. |
| 11 | **Origen** three times (in different forms) makes use of the phrase ἀπολυθήσεται τοῦ περισπασμοῦ, "doubts will be solved," which is found in this scholion. Notably the phrase, in any form, is not used by any other writer, Christian or otherwise. Origen also uses the term "common death," as found in this scholion, in his *Commentary on Matthew* 13.9. |

| Scholia | Parallels between the *Scholia* and Ancient Authors |
|---|---|
| 12 | **Origen** parallels content in this scholion in his *Commentary on John* 1.229 (which is paralleled by Scholion 6), *Homilies on Luke* 13.4–6 (which is also paralleled by Scholia 6 and 30). The scholion seems connected with Scholion 6 on the basis of their shared content. |
| 13 | The phrase οὐκ ἀπογνωστέον, "one must not reject," is used in this form around a dozen times before the tenth century by Christian writers; two of these uses are by **Origen** and three by **Didymus**. Didymus also twice mirrors the usage in this example, where he juxtaposes the noted phrase while mentioning, respectively, heretics or false teachers. The lexeme ψευδόμαντις, "false teacher," is not used by Origen, but is used by Didymus 4 times, though many other authors also use it. |
| 14 | |
| 15 | **Origen** closely parallels content in this scholion in his *Commentary on John* 2.56–57 and *Homilies on Genesis* 1.13 (which is also paralleled in Scholia 30 and 36). Other parallels with Origen can be found in his *First Principles* 1.1.2; 2.10.4. The content of this scholion seems also related to the first part of Scholion 30. |
| 16 | |
| 17 | **Origen**, more than a dozen times, uses variations of the phrase οὐ φύσεως ἀπολλυμένης, "not of the nature of destruction," which is found in this scholion. No other Christian author uses the phrase, though the author of *De Trinitate* 2.6.9.3 (TLG #2102.009), perhaps **Didymus**, uses a slight variant of it once. This scholion seems to be contradicting Gnostic ideas that some people were damned by nature, which could place the scholion in the second or the third century. See, for example, Origen's discussion of this idea when describing the beliefs of the Valentinian Heracleon; Origen, *Commentary on John* 13.63–64, 92. Similar Gnostic and Manichaean ideas, however, were also a concern to some Christian writers in later centuries. |
| 18 | **Didymus** uses this scholion's phrase δυνάμενοι φάναι, "who are able to say," in this exact form three times, though **Cyril of Alexandria** does use a variant of it once; see Tzamalikos, *An Ancient Commentary*, 275. |

| Scholia | Parallels between the *Scholia* and Ancient Authors |
|---|---|
| 19 | **Didymus** and **Origen** each make use of the lexeme ἀσυντρόχαστος, which is found in this scholion. They are the only Christian authors to use this lexeme. |
| 20 | **Origen** parallels content in this scholion in his *Homilies on Exodus* 12.4 (also paralleled by Scholion 27). This scholion also directly parallels Scholion 27 because they both draw upon the account in Luke 24 to make the same theological point. |
| 21 | **Didymus** parallels content in this scholion in *Fragmenta in Psalmos (e commentario altero)*, Psalm 74.4, 7, Fragment 781A–782A (TLG #2102.021). This scholion also seems related to Scholion 22 because these two scholia emphasize that both the Church and Christ are firmly established. |
| 22 | **Didymus** the Blind closely parallels this passage in his *Commentary on Zechariah* 1.153–154 (TLG #2102.010, pp. 59–60 in Hill). This scholion appears related to Scholion 26 because they both discuss the deity of Christ. The scholion may also be related to Scholion 21 because they (Scholia 21 and 22) emphasize that both the Church and Christ are firmly established. Finally, the scholion may also reflect fourth-century anti-Arian concerns, but such issues were also discussed earlier and later in the Christian era. |
| 23 | |
| 24 | |
| 25 | |
| 26 | This scholion may be related to Scholion 22 because they both discuss the deity of Christ. The scholion may also reflect fourth-century anti-Arian concerns, but such issues were also discussed earlier and later in the Christian era. Furthermore, Tzamalikos notes that the only Christian author to use the construction ὅθεν οὐκ + adjective is **Didymus;** see Tzamalikos, *An Ancient Commentary*, 147. |
| 27 | **Origen** parallels content in this scholion in his *Homilies on Exodus* 12.4 (also paralleled by Scholion 20) and his *Commentary on the Psalms* 1.1 (PG 12: 1077). This scholion also parallels Scholion 20 directly because they both draw upon the account in Luke 24 to make the same theological point. |

| Scholia | Parallels between the *Scholia* and Ancient Authors |
|---|---|
| 28 | Tzamalikos notes that the phrase μετὰ τὸ ἐγνωκέναι, "after I recognized," occurs in this exact form only in **Origen**, *Exhortation to Martyrdom* 32.11; see Tzamalikos, *An Ancient Commentary*, 329.<br><br>**Didymus** closely parallels the content of the scholion in his *Commentarii in Psalmos* 22–26.10, page 107 lines 22–25 (TLG #2102.017). This scholion shares thematic content with Scholion 9. |
| 29 | **Origen** in *Against Celsus* 8.17 quotes from Rv 5.8 and juxtaposes it with Psalm 141.2, just as this scholion does. |
| 30 | No author before the tenth century makes use of the idiom τὸ δὲ ὅμοιον νόει, "in the same way consider," in any form except **Origen**, who uses it three times; see Tzamalikos, *An Ancient Commentary*, 356. The scholion also parallels content found in Origen's *Commentary on John* 1.281–282; *Against Celsus* 4.72; *Commentary on Romans* 1.16.3; *Homilies on Genesis* 1.13 (also paralleled by Scholia 15 and 36); *Homilies on Numbers* 20.3.6–7; 20.4.2; 14.2.9; 11.4.5; *Homilies on Luke* 13.4–6 (also paralleled by Scholia 6 and 12). The first part of this scholion seems also related to Scholion 15. |
| 31 | **Didymus** parallels the content of this scholion in Didymus, *Commentary on Zechariah* 3.67–73 (TLG #2102.010, pp. 200–201 of Hill 2006), where he refers readers to an exegetical work of his on the Apocalypse that seems remarkably similar to this scholion. Tzamalikos notes that Didymus uses squared numbers elsewhere in his exegesis; Tzamalikos, *An Ancient Commentary*, 369. The scholion also makes use of the phrase τοὺς ἐγχειρισθέντας τὰ ἐπίπονα, "those who have been entrusted with the labors," which is used in a slightly different form only by Didymus; see Tzamalikos, *An Ancient Commentary*, 360. **Origen** in his *Commentary on John* 1.4–8 loosely parallels the content of the scholion. The content of this scholion overlaps with Scholion 32, likely because they deal with the same subject matter. |
| 32 | **Origen** remarkably parallels content in this scholion in his *Homilies on Exodus* 1.2 and *Commentary on John* 1.4–8. The content of this scholion overlaps with Scholion 31, likely because they deal with the same subject matter. The scholion also seems to be excerpted from a work specifically concerned with the Apocalypse. |

| Scholia | Parallels between the *Scholia* and Ancient Authors |
|---------|------------------------------------------------------|
| 33 | Tzamalikos notes phrasing in this scholion that is used only by **Philo of Alexandria;** see Tzamalikos, *An Ancient Commentary*, 382. Because Philo cannot actually have been the author of the scholion, such an observation shows the slippery nature of identifying authorship simply on the basis of shared thought and word usage. |
| 34 | |
| 35 | |
| 36 | An impressive parallel can be found between this scholion and **Origen's** *Homilies on the Psalms*, Ps. 76 hom. 4.2–3, where Origen also speaks of a wheel with thunder in it and correlates it to the seven thunders of Revelation and to Is 11.2 as well as to the fact that John and James were called the Sons of Thunder. Other less impressive parallels with Origen can be found when he quotes from Rv 10.4 and compares it with Jn 21.25, as this scholion does, in his *Commentary on John* 5.3; 13.27–28, 33, but here he does not correlate the seven thunders to the seven spirits of wisdom. Elsewhere, in *Commentary on John* 1.147, 13.33, and *Homilies on Jeremiah* 8.5.2, Origen does talk about the seven spirits of wisdom, but does not correlate them with the seven thunders of Rv 10.4. Origen further, albeit vaguely, parallels content in this scholion in his *Homilies on Genesis* 1.13 (also paralleled by Scholia 15 and 30).<br><br>**Didymus** correlates the seven spirits of wisdom with a different passage from Revelation in his *Commentary on Zechariah* 1.278–282 (TLG #2102.010, pp. 85–86 of Hill 2006). In his *Commentary on Zechariah* 1.254 (TLG #2102.010, pp. 80–81 of Hill 2006) Didymus also refers to the seven spirits of wisdom as they relate to the seven eyes on the stone in Zechariah 3.9. |
| 37 | |
| 38a | |
| 38b | This scholion is an excerpt from **Irenaeus,** *Against Heresies* 5.28.2–4, 29.1–2. |
| 39 | This scholion is an excerpt from **Irenaeus,** *Against Heresies* 5.30.3. |

# TRANSLATION

*ANONYMOUS GREEK SCHOLIA*
*ON THE APOCALYPSE*

*The Apocalypse of the Holy John the Theologian*

I.

EVELATION 1.1: *The Apocalypse of Jesus Christ, which God gave to him to show to his slaves what must soon come to be, and he signified it, having sent it through his angel to his slave John,*

What was spoken by the Savior to his acquaintances, "I shall no longer call you slaves, but friends,"[1] does not disagree with what was confessed by them concerning themselves, that they were slaves of the Lord. For though in giving to them honor and preeminence he calls them "friends," "children," and "brothers,"[2] they themselves, however, since they are grateful, confess that they are slaves and consider that they have a worthy and mighty God as a Master. Indeed, in the epistles which they wrote, just as others prefix the highest ranks of mortals, they prefix to the beginning [of their letters] this same [rank of slave]. And James and Paul and the rest consistently affix to the beginning [of their letters] the very same thing.[3] For not insisting on their full rights on account of their humility, they are silent concerning what has been clearly written about their great rank.[4]

1. Jn 15.15.
2. Mt 12.48–50, 25.40; Mk 10.24; Lk 12.4; Jn 13.33, 15.13–15.
3. Cf. Jas 1.1; Rom 1.1; Phil 1.1; Ti 1.1; 2 Pt 1.1; Jude 1.1.
4. According to the TLG database, Didymus is the only Christian author before the tenth century to make use of the lexeme ἐλαττωτικός ("not insisting on full rights") in any form. Like the *Scholia*, Didymus also uses the lexeme with the genitive reflexive pronoun. Origen similarly explains why the apostles called themselves

2.

Revelation 1.2: ... *who testified the word of God and the testimony of Jesus Christ, as much as he saw.*

He said that the *testimony* was the proclamation of what has been made known and the disclosure of the word concerning them.

3.

Revelation 1.3–4a: *Blessed is the one who reads and blessed are they who hear the words of the prophecy and they who keep the things which are written in it.* (4a) *For the time is near. John, to the seven churches that are in Asia. Grace to you and peace from God.*

Divine Scripture universally blesses the godly and great, but not the small and human. Therefore, also in this place *those who read and they who hear are blessed*, not as though one must [simply] happen to hear what is set forth. For to *read* intelligently, and not to *hear* superficially, but faithfully, renders one *blessed*. And from the text that is set before us, we learn that, since John is a prophet, then along with this he is an apostle and evangelist.[5] For prophecy is the yokefellow of the prophet.

4.

Revelation 1.4b–7: *He who is and who was and who is coming, and from the seven spirits that are before his throne,* (5) *and from Jesus Christ, the faithful witness, firstborn from the dead and ruler of the kings of the earth. To him who loved us and washed us from our sins in his blood,* (6) *and made us a royal priesthood to our God and his Father; glory and power be to him forever and ever. Amen.* (7) *Behold, he comes with the clouds, and every eye and those who pierced him shall see him, and all the tribes of the earth shall mourn him. Yes, Amen.*

---

"slaves" in his *Commentary on Romans* 1.1.1, though he uses different biblical passages in support of the idea.

5. In this scholion the author gives John the titles of apostle, evangelist, and prophet. Origen does likewise in his *Commentary on John* 2.45, and according to the TLG database he is the only Christian author to list these titles in close association with the name John.

The Word embraces three tenses. John the Theologian,[6] who perceived this, here says that the Savior is *He who is and who was and who is coming.* The [phrase] *"who is"* brings forward the present; the [phrase] *"who was"* [brings forward] what has passed; and the [phrase] *"who is coming"* [brings forward] the future. Having understood such things concerning the Word, the apostle, perceiving him to be Christ, says, "Jesus Christ is the same yesterday, today, and forever."[7] Now, "yesterday" brings forward what has passed; "today" [brings forward] what is present; and "forever" [brings forward] the future.[8]

## 5.

Revelation 1.8–16a: *"I am the Alpha and the Omega,[9] the Beginning and the End," says the Lord God, "who is and who was and who is coming, the Almighty."* (9) *I, John, your brother and partner in the tribulation and [in] the kingdom and the patience [which are] in Christ Jesus, was on the island that is called Patmos on account of the word of God and on account of the testimony of Jesus Christ.* (10) *I was in the Spirit on the Lord's Day, and I heard a great voice behind me like a trumpet* (11) *saying, "What you see write in a book and send to the seven churches, to Ephesus and to Smyrna and to Pergamum and to Thyatira, and to Sardis and to Philadelphia and to Laodicea."* (12) *And then I turned to see the voice that was speaking with me. And having turned, I beheld seven golden lampstands* (13) *and in the midst of the seven lampstands [there was one] like a son of man, who was clothed in a long robe, and around his chest was wrapped a golden belt,* (14) *and his head and hair were white like white wool, like snow, and his eyes were like a flame of fire,* (15) *and his feet were like burnished bronze, like that which is refined in the furnace, and his voice was like the sound of many waters,* (16a) *and he had in his right hand seven stars.*

6. Θεολόγος. Christians do not make use of this word until the fourth century. Origen uses this term in *Fragmenta in evangelium Joannis (in catenis)*, Fragment 1, Line 27 (TLG #2042.006), but this example comes from a catena and therefore could easily be a later addition. Didymus makes use of it once in *De Trinitate* 1.15.4 (TLG #2102.008), but this may not have been written by him. For a useful discussion on this term, see Tzamalikos, *An Ancient Commentary*, 214–18.

7. Heb 13.8.

8. Origen makes very similar statements in *On Prayer* 27.13, but such sentiments are found in other authors as well; see Tzamalikos, *An Ancient Commentary*, 218–19.

9. Literally: "the α and the ω."

The Son is not simply one as in [made up of] one thing, nor many as in [made up of] parts, but he is one as in [made up of] all things. Hence also, to put it another way, all things are one. For he is the circle of all powers which are enclosed and united into one. On account of this, the Word is called *"the Alpha and the Omega"*;[10] not only does the end become the beginning [in a circle], it also finishes [the circle] again, and thus it does not receive any separation from the earlier[11] beginning. Therefore, to believe in him and through him[12] is to become a unity, being continuously united in him. But to lack faith is doubt, separation, and division.[13]

## 6.

Revelation 1.16b–17a: *And from his mouth proceeded a double-edged sword, and his appearance was like the sun shining in its power.* (17a) *And when I beheld him, I fell at his feet as though dead.*

In Psalm 56 it is written, "The sons of men, their teeth are weapons and arrows, and their tongue is a sharp sword."[14] For this reason what was spoken [in the passage] is not at all blameworthy. For if weapons of the righteous, choice arrows and a praiseworthy sword, are used by all the sons of men to wage war[15]—[some] for both God and righteousness, and [others] for the evil one and sin— then it is necessary not to dispute what was spoken here of how a son of man had *a two-edged sword in [his] mouth.* For he himself said, "I have not come to bring peace on the earth, but a sword,"[16] such that "it pierces to the division of soul and spirit," etc.[17] So the ignoble who have meditated on false doctrines, have sufficiently sharpened [their] tongues as a sharp sword for the evil of the listeners, but they who have sharpened [their] mind in the divine Scriptures on behalf of the salvation of both themselves and their listeners,

10. Literally: "the α and the ω."
11. ἄνωθεν, which could also be rendered "higher" or "again."
12. Cf. Col 1.16.
13. This scholion comes from Clement of Alexandria, *Stromateis* 4.25.156–57.
14. Ps 56.5. Psalm numbering is from the LXX.
15. Literally: "praiseworthy sword of all the sons of men who wage war."
16. Mt 10.34.
17. Heb 4.12.

they have a tongue that becomes a *sharp* sword for salvation. For the ignoble wound with a sword, but the tongues of the wise heal and wound in love.[18] And so the Lord wounded us in love.[19]

7.

Revelation 1.17b: *And he placed his right hand upon me, saying, "Do not fear; I am the first and the last."*

Such a one who understands the divine visions anagogically understands God the Word to be the *Alpha*, *a beginning* and cause of all things, *first* not in time, but in honor.[20] For glory and honor are offered to him[21] that in the consummation of the ages, when he ushers in the *end* for [all] those things that he has done, he might be said to be the *Omega*.[22] And *"first and last,"* again not according to time, but as ushering in a *beginning and an end*. For, as *a beginning and an end*, the uttermost letters[23] [of the alphabet] are included, and the other intervening [letters] are embraced [as well]. But in this way, though being life according to nature, he became dead for us. Hav-

---

18. Cf. Prv 12.18.

19. Cf. Song 2.5; 5.8. Origen's *Commentary on John* 1.229 parallels this scholion both in its general content and in that it draws upon the same passages from the Gospel of Matthew, the Epistle to the Hebrews, and the Song of Songs. Other parallels can be found in Origen, *Homilies on the Psalms*, Ps. 36 hom. 3.3 and Ps. 76 hom. 3.5. This scholion also parallels Origen's *Homilies on Luke* 13.4–6, the same passage paralleled by Scholia 12 and 30. This scholion seems further connected with Scholion 12 on the basis of their shared content. Tzamalikos (*An Ancient Commentary*, 224) does note other, though less impressive, parallels with authors like Didymus and Theodoret.

20. Tzamalikos argues that "first not in time" reflects the understanding of Didymus. But while Didymus does use similar terminology, he never applies it to Christ. Didymus does, however, vaguely parallel thoughts in this scholion when he discusses the same passage in the Apocalypse in his *Commentary on Ecclesiastes*, 11–12, P. 328. See Tzamalikos, *An Ancient Commentary*, 227.

21. Harnack claims there is a lacuna here; Turner is not so sure.

22. Literally: "ω." Harnack, Wohlenberg, Stählin, and Turner all found this sentence to be textually corrupt and quite difficult to understand. See C. H. Turner, "The Text of the Newly Discovered Scholia of Origen on the Apocalypse," *The Journal of Theological Studies* 13, no. 51 (1912): 388, https://doi.org/10.1093/jts/os-XIII.51.386.

23. στοιχείων or "elements."

ing loosed the pains of death,[24] he is *alive forever.*[25] And he confessed to having become dead and to not being life,[26] yet he affirmed, saying, *"I am he who lives and became dead, and behold, I am alive."*[27] Such is why he appointed himself to endure the state of death, yet also [he appointed himself] to be life forever. The one who has learned such letters—I am speaking of *Alpha and Omega,*[28] not the material [letters of the alphabet], but those which the Holy Spirit writes— knows that he is *a beginning* of the universe and *an end* of all things, according to what was spoken by John the Theologian himself, "In the beginning was the Word,"[29] and the "Word became flesh,"[30] for, having become incarnate, he became *the completion*[31] of the salvation of the universe.[32]

8.

Revelation 1.18– 20a: *"I am he who lives and became dead, and behold, I am alive forever and ever, Amen! And I have the keys of death and of Hades. (19) Therefore, write what you saw and what is and what is about to be after these things. (20a) The mystery of the seven stars that you saw in my right hand and the seven golden lampstands: the seven stars are angels of the seven churches."*

For *he who became dead* concluded his life upon the earth, so that he, having been taken up, "might sit at the right hand of the Majesty on high"[33] to *live forever,* since "death no longer has dominion,"[34]

24. Cf. Acts 2.24.
25. Rv 1.18.
26. Cf. Jn 14.6.
27. Rv 1.18.
28. Literally: "the α and the ω." Here and throughout this scholion the author makes use of titles of Christ found in Rv 1.8; 21.6; 22.13.
29. Jn 1.1.
30. Jn 1.14.
31. Literally: "the end."
32. This scholion, which uses the fourth-century phrase "John the Theologian" (see note on Scholion 4 above), appears to have fourth-century theology associated with it and is perhaps Arian. Furthermore, the scholion correlates the term "Alpha" with "beginning" and "first," and likewise the term "Omega" with "end" and "last," whereas in Origen's *Commentary on John* 1.209 he cautions not to do so. *Contra* this scholion, Origen also implies that the Son is eternal; see *Commentary on John* 1.204.
33. Heb 1.3.
34. Rom 6.9.

because "he who lives, lives" *forever* "to God,"[35] not dying anymore.

9.

Revelation 1.20b–2.3: *"And the seven lampstands are the seven churches. (2.1) To the angel of the church in Ephesus, write: These things says he who holds the seven stars in his right hand, who walks in the midst of the seven golden lampstands. (2) 'I know your works and your toil and your patience and that you are not able to bear the wicked, and you have tested those who say they are apostles and are not, and you found them to be liars. (3) And you have patience and have suffered on account of my name and have not grown weary.'"*

All the present age is named "night" according to the [symbolic] sense, as the parable of the ten virgins makes clear.[36] And so, since the sun shines at day and not at night, there must be lamplight for those who live at night. And this is that which enlightens those who obey godly instruction. And since it is necessary for lamplight[37] to be nowhere else but in the *churches*, he named the churches "*lampstands*," placing them under the number *seven*, which is mystical, and therefore holy and blessed.[38] He who applies his own mind to the true light thereby lights his [mind] like such a lamp so that he who has lit the lamp might therefore help those who are in need, and might place [the lamp] upon the uttered word as upon a *lampstand*. Thus, he shall enlighten with teaching those who have not yet had the opportunity[39] to be illuminated by the true sun.[40] For they alone, who walk nobly as in the day[41] and rejoice, perceive this, so that they might see the day of the Savior. And if some who have a nocturnal existence lack this [sun], they might still be enlightened by a lamp from [the churches].

---

35. Rom 6.10.
36. Cf. Mt 25.1–13.
37. Literally: "it."
38. Regarding the number seven being "holy and blessed," see Scholion 28 and notes.
39. καιρόν or "time."
40. Cf. Mal 4.2.
41. Cf. 1 Thes 5.5, 8.

10.

Revelation 2.4–7a: "*But I have this against you, that you have forsaken your first love. (5) And so remember from where you have fallen and repent and do your first works. But if not, I will come to you, and I will take your lampstand from its place if you do not repent. (6) But you have this [in your favor], that you hate the works of the Nicolaitans, which I also hate. (7) He who has ears let him hear ...*"

[The following statement], "*I know your works and toil and patience, which have been performed with love,*"[42] does not disagree with [the statement] "*but I have this against you, that you have forsaken your first love.*" For [these two phrases] would quarrel with one another, if [the angel] were charging them with completely rejecting love. But the adjacent phrase, "*you have forsaken your first love,*" does not permit one to understand this [in that manner]. For possibly a slackening and a lessening had occurred concerning his loving disposition.[43] Therefore, even after [love] had been abandoned, he [still] possessed *toil and works and patience* which were known by God. For he who is performing a deed virtuously does not necessarily perform it in a permanent habitual way.

11.

Revelation 2.7b–12a: "*... what the Spirit says to the churches. To him who overcomes I shall give to him to eat from the tree of life, which is in the paradise of my God. (8) And to the angel of the church in Smyrna, write: 'These things says the First and the Last, who became dead and lives: (9) I know your works and tribulation and poverty, but you are rich, and the blasphemy of those who say they are Jews, and are not, but are a synagogue of Satan. (10) Do not be afraid of what you are about to suffer. Behold, the devil is about to put [some] from among you into prison, so that you may be tested, and you shall have tribulation for ten days. Be faithful unto death, and I shall give to you the crown of life. (11) He who has ears, let him hear what the Spirit says to the churches. He*

---

42. Rv 2.2.
43. Didymus uses the lexeme of ἀγαπητικός, "loving disposition," seven times; however, it is not used at all by Origen. It is, though, used by many other authors, including Clement of Alexandria.

*who overcomes shall not be wronged by the second death.'* (12a) *And to the angel of the church in Pergamum, write:"*

It is possible to say that the first death is that to which a composite creature is subjected, which custom calls "common death."[44] But after this the *second [death]* follows sin, which "when it is completed brings forth death."[45] And so *he who conquers* shall be *tested* with the first [death], "since it is appointed for all men to die once."[46] But he shall be beyond the *second [death]* on account of [his] innocence in order that *he may not be wronged by it* [which means] he shall not be injured. Furthermore, someone [may] call the *second death* a "punishment" according to what has been spoken, "Soul and body shall be destroyed in hell."[47] This has the same meaning as, "The one who destroys his temple shall be destroyed by God."[48] But *he [who conquers]* is not at all *wronged* by this *second death*. Now should anyone think that this [second death] is impossible to understand concerning an *angel*, he will have his doubts solved[49] when he recognizes that every rational nature is capable of receiving the above given meanings of [the second] death. Perhaps he who is troubled by this suffers perplexity because he was thinking in [his] mind of the common death.

### 12.

Revelation 2.12a–14: *"These things says he who has the sharp double-edged sword. (13) 'I know your works and where you dwell, where the throne of Satan is. And you hold my name, and you did not deny my faith even in the days [of]*[50] *Antipas, my martyr, my faithful one, who was killed among you, where*

44. Origen also uses the term "common death," as found in this scholion, in his *Commentary on Matthew* 13.9.

45. Jas 1.15.

46. Heb 9.27.

47. Mt 10.28.

48. 1 Cor 3.17.

49. ἀπολυθήσεται τοῦ περισπασμοῦ, "doubts will be solved." This is a phrase of Origen, and it is found in different forms in three locations in his writings: *Contra Celsum*, Book 7, section 1, line 13, and Book 7, section 28, line 47 (Borret TLG # 2042.001); and *Commentarii in epistulam ad Romanos* (1.1–12.21) (*in catenis*) (Ramsbotham TLG # 2042.036). According to the TLG database, this phrase, in any form, is not used by any other writers, Christian or otherwise.

50. Literally: "days which."

*Satan lives.* (14) *But I have a few things against you, that you have there those who hold the teaching of Balaam, who taught Balak to cast a stumbling block before the sons of Israel and to eat food sacrificed to idols and to commit sexual immorality.*"

The *double-edged sword* which proceeds from the mouth of the Savior is his divine teaching, concerning which in the Gospels he also says, "I have not come to bring peace, but a sword."[51] [This sword] is said to be *double-edged* since it is able to cut on both sides, for it cuts not only the very spawn of evil, but also the false doctrines of the prideful. In the same way then, he proclaims these things to those in Pergamum who have among themselves the teaching of the prophet Balaam and the Nicolaitans. For with the Word it is necessary to cut off and destroy the deceiving sophistries of heretics.[52]

13.

Revelation 2.15–17a: "*So you likewise have those who hold the teaching of the Nicolaitans.* (16) *Repent! But if not, I will come to you quickly and will war against them with the sword of my mouth.* (17a) *He who has ears, let him hear what the Spirit says to the churches.*"

One must refer the historical events [in this passage] to the deceivers evidenced here, who lead them, anagogically [speaking], to sexual impurity and idolatry. Such are many of the heretics. One must not reject that these things are also said concerning certain fleshless false teachers, for this was shown to the apostle through a revelation.[53]

51. Mt 10.34.
52. This scholion seems to be linked with Scholion 6 on the basis of its content. Scholion 6 and this scholion also parallel Origen's *Commentary on John* 1.229. When the thoughts of Scholia 6 and 12 are combined, they form a striking parallel with Origen's *Homily on Luke* 13.4–6, the same passage paralleled in Scholion 30. But see the footnotes for Scholion 6 for potential parallels with other authors.
53. The phrase οὐκ ἀπογνωστέον, "one must not reject," is used in this lexile form around a dozen times before the 10th century by Christian writers, twice by Origen and three times by Didymus. Didymus also mirrors the usage in this example twice where he juxtaposes the noted phrase while mentioning, respectively, heretics or false teachers in his *Commentarii in Zachariam*, Book 1, section 393, lines

14.

Revelation 2.17a–18a: "*To him who conquers, I shall give to him to eat of the hidden manna, and I shall give to him a white stone, and upon the stone a new name written, which no one knows except him who receives [it]*. (18) *And to the angel of the church in Thyatira, write:*"

"Moses did not give bread to you," said the Lord to the ignorant Jews, "but the Father shall give true bread. This is the bread of God, that whoever eats from it shall not die."[54] This is *the hidden manna. "And upon the stone a new name,"* but since the Word concerns spiritual things, one must proceed higher, beyond any sensible manifestation concerning [this] *stone*. Therefore, on the spiritual *stone*, [which is] white on account of [its] radiance, a *new name is written* according to the New Covenant, which symbolizes the quality of the one who received it and knows it. [This is the case] because at every rank a man has a title suitable to the quality of [his] rank, since previous names always pass away. *The name that is written* all over the one who is perfected has no other after it; it is [therefore] always *new* according to how the New Covenant has no successor. And indeed this *new name* is indicative of the "hidden man of the heart";[55] *no one knows it except only him who receives [it]*, which corresponds to [the saying] "For who knows the things of a man?" etc.[56]

15.

Revelation 2.18a–20a: "*These things says the Son of God, who has eyes*[57] *like flames of fire, and his feet are like burnished bronze.* (19) *'I know your works and love and faith and service and your patience and [that] your last works are greater than your first.* (20a) *But I have this against you: that you allow your woman ...*'"

---

2–3, and Book 4, section 84, lines 1–2 (Doutreleau TLG #2102.010). The lexeme φευδόμαντις, "false teacher," is not used by Origen, but is used by Didymus four times, though many other authors also use it.

54. Jn 6.32–33, 50.
55. 1 Pt 3.4.
56. 1 Cor 2.11.
57. Literally: "who has his eyes."

Through the passage [John] reveals the sublimely mysterious, overseeing, and pervasive power of the Son of God over the universe. And since through [his] gaze he destroys and withers base things, his *eyes* are called a *flame of fire*. For they consume all depraved behavior, as it has been named, "wood, hay, and straw."[58] Concerning this powerful guardian it is written, "He who looks upon the earth and makes it tremble."[59] For after God has gazed, all the material elements are routed from those who have [such in their] minds. But also his *feet*, on which he journeys, penetrating every place, are compared to *burnished bronze* on account of the fact that divine incense[60] is *bronze* in so far as it descends to creatures. This is because, while he walks, he makes a certain clang that, according to providential action, wakes those who sleep.[61]

16.

Revelation 2.20b: "… *Jezebel, who says she is a prophet and teaches and deceives my slaves to commit sexual immorality and to eat that which is sacrificed to idols.*"

Be careful not to apply the name of *Jezebel* to the opinion and heresy of the Nicolaitans given that [it is rather] the works of that opinion which are attached to Jezebel, who tries to drag [men] into sexual immorality and the use of *food* sacrificed to idols. For this [reason] he calls her a *woman* because she is passionate and effeminate.[62]

17.

Revelation 2.21–28: "*And I gave her time, so that she might repent, and she did not want to repent from her sexual immorality.* (22) *Behold, I shall cast*

---

58. 1 Cor 3.12.

59. Ps 103.32.

60. χαλκολιβάνου, "burnished bronze," contains the word λίβανος, "incense," within it.

61. Ideas in this scholion are closely similar to Origen's *Commentary on John* 2.56–57 and *Homilies on Genesis* 1.13, the latter of which is also paralleled in Scholia 30 and 36. Other parallels with Origen can be found in *First Principles* 1.1.2; 2.10.4. The content of this scholion also parallels the beginning of Scholion 30.

62. Origen mentions this passage from the Apocalypse in his *Homilies on Numbers* 20.1.6, but only vaguely parallels this scholion.

*her on a bed; and those who commit adultery with her [I shall cast] into great tribulation, unless they shall repent from her works. (23) And I shall kill her children unto death, and all the churches shall know that I am he who searches minds and hearts and I shall give to each of you according to your works. (24) But I say to you who remain in Thyatira, as many as do not have this teaching, who do not know 'the depths of Satan,' as they say, I shall not lay upon you another burden. (25) Only hold what you have until I shall come. (26) And he who conquers and he who keeps my works until the end, I shall give to him authority over the nations, (27) and he shall shepherd them with an iron staff, he shall shatter them as clay vessels, (28a) as also I have received from my Father."*

Since a time of patience was granted by the Judge, in which it was possible for her to *repent*, if Jezebel wished, she is [hence] not of the nature of destruction.[63]

18.

Revelation 2.28b–3.1a: *"And I shall give to him the Morningstar. (29) He who has ears let him hear what the Spirit says to the churches. (3.1a) And to the angel of the church in Sardis ..."*

In addition to *authority*, which he who keeps godly *works* until the end receives,[64] the *Morningstar* is [also] given by the Savior to him, which is light that shines before the Sun of Righteousness rises.[65] They who are illuminated by it are able to say truly,[66] "The

---

63. οὐ φύσεως ἀπολλυμένης, "not of a nature of destruction." This is a favorite phrase of Origen, who uses variations of it over a dozen times while Didymus uses a slight variant of it once, in his *De Trinitate* 2.6.9.3 (Seiler TLG #2102.009), which may not have been written by him. This scholion seems to be contradicting Gnostic ideas that some people were damned by nature, which could place the scholion in the second or third century. See, for example, Origen's discussion of this idea when describing the beliefs of the Valentinian Heracleon; Origen, *Commentary on John* 13.63–64, 92. Similar Gnostic and Manichaean ideas, however, were also a concern to some Christian writers in later centuries.

64. Rv 2.26.

65. Cf. Mal 4.2.

66. Didymus uses the phrase δυνάμενοι φάναι, "who are able to say," in its exact form three times, though Cyril of Alexandria does also use a variant of it once; see Tzamalikos, *An Ancient Commentary*, 275.

night is far gone, and the day is near,"[67] and, "I shall awaken the dawn."[68]

19.

Revelation 3.1b–7a: "... *Write: These things says he who has the seven spirits of God and the seven stars. I know your works, that you have a name, and that you are alive, though you are dead. (2) Be watchful and strengthen the remaining things that are about to die. For I have not found your works complete before my God. (3) Therefore, remember how you received and heard [these things], and keep [them], and repent. But*[69] *if you are not watchful, I shall come as a thief, and you shall not know at what hour I shall come upon you. (4) But you have a few names in Sardis, which have not stained their clothes, and they shall walk with me in white, because they are worthy. (5) He who conquers in this way shall be enrobed in white clothes, and I shall not blot out his name from the book of life, and I shall confess his name before my Father and before his angels. (6) He who has ears, let him hear what the Spirit says to the churches. (7a) And to the angel of the church in Philadelphia, write:*"

Since now the teaching has been proclaimed to the seven churches that have been specified, be aware that *the seven spirits* are not shares of the Spirit, since each church has a fellowship that is distinct[70] in regard to that of other [churches]. You must [also] consistently understand the *seven spirits* to be the *seven stars*, with each star symbolizing the illumination of a particular church. It is possible [as well] to interpret the *seven stars* as the seven angels of the seven churches.

20.

Revelation 3.7b–11: "*These things says the true angel, who has the key of David, who opens and no one shall shut it and who shuts and no one opens,*

---

67. Rom 13.12.

68. Ps 107.3.

69. Literally: "and so."

70. According to the TLG database ἀσυντρόχαστος, "distinct," is used only three other times in all of Greek literature in any form: once by Origen, *De oratione*, Chapter 24, section 2, line 6 (Mühlenberg TLG #2102.021); once by Didymus, *Commentarii in Psalmos* 20–21 (Doutreleau, Gesche, and Gronewald TLG #2102.016); and once by a secular writer, Simplicius.

*except him who opens and no one shall shut.*[71] (8) *I know your works; behold, I have set before you an opened door, which no one is able to shut, because you have little power and have kept my word and have not denied my name. (9) Behold, I put forward from the synagogue of Satan those who say they are Jews, and are not, but lie. Behold, I shall make them so that they shall come and shall worship before your feet and shall know that I have loved you. (10) Because you have kept the word of my patience, I also shall keep you from the hour of trial, which is about to come upon the whole world, to test those who dwell upon the earth. (11) I am coming quickly, hold what you have, so that no one may take your crown.*"

"*Holy, true,*"[72] not through participation, but being such in essence. He himself is God the Word,[73] *having the key of David.* For when the Word became flesh,[74] he opens the Scriptures by this *key* [Scriptures], which were shut before [his] advent [and] which *no one is able to shut* by asserting that they have not been fulfilled. This one opened them to those with Cleopas as he journeyed together [with them] on the way.[75] But since he opened them, having fulfilled them through [his] departure,[76] he shut the shadow of the Law,[77] having put the Jews outside of Jerusalem. Therefore, no one shall open that which is according to the letter of the Law, which no longer has a place to be kept. He [instead] *opens* what is possible for men to understand, but he *shuts* as much as what is not possible [for them] to know in the present life.[78]

71. This verse has a number of unique textual variants.

72. The text quoted is different from the text of the Apocalypse given previously.

73. Cf. Jn 1.1.

74. Cf. Jn 1.14.

75. Cf. Lk 24.13–35. This scholion parallels material in Origen's *Homilies on Exodus* 12.4, which is paralleled by Scholion 27. Additionally, this scholion also directly parallels Scholion 27 because they both draw upon the account in Lk 24 to make the same theological point.

76. Tzamalikos (*An Ancient Commentary*, 281) points out that Didymus is the only author who uses the phrase δι' ἐκβάσεως, "through [his] departure," in this precise form. Tzamalikos is correct that Didymus does make use of it twice, but several other Christian authors, including Origen, use variations of it, according to the TLG database.

77. Cf. Heb 10.1.

78. Turner believes that this last sentence is a gloss from a previous scribe, partially because there are several words that do not make sense and partially because

21.

Revelation 3.12a: *"He who conquers, I shall make for him a pillar in the temple of my God."*

We find that all who are named *pillars* are able to bear the most important things of the Church. Therefore, Paul has indeed said that James and Cephas and John are pillars.[79] And God says concerning such ones, "I have strengthened her pillars."[80] Since they are also built up by wings of piety and virtue, it is indeed said concerning those who will bear the image of heavenly [man],[81] "the pillars of heaven are prostrate."[82] And since each of them who thus are *pillars in the temple of God* is steadfast and immovable, rooted and established in love,[83] then they may never be outside, where Cain was, having gone out from the face of God.[84] For the one [who is a *pillar*] is not cast outside, since he comes to the Savior through works of virtue.[85] Upon him who has thus become a *pillar*, he *writes the name* of the Father, having engraved the knowledge of the Father on him, but also the *name of the city* of the living God, which is the heavenly *Jerusalem*,[86] *which has descended from God out of heaven*.[87] This is the Church of the living God.[88]

---

Turner regards this as something that does not fit within the preceding paragraph and does not belong to Origen's theology; see Turner, "The Text of the Newly Discovered Scholia of Origen on the Apocalypse," 393.

79. Cf. Gal 2.9.

80. Ps 74.4.

81. Cf. 1 Cor 15.49.

82. Jb 26.11.

83. Cf. Eph 3.17.

84. Cf. Gn 4.16.

85. Cf. Jn 6.37.

86. Cf. Heb 12.22.

87. Rv 3.12; 21.2. This and previous quotations from the Apocalypse are taken from the next section of the Apocalypse.

88. Cf. 1 Tm 3.15. This scholion seems related to Scholion 22 because these two scholia emphasize that both the Church and Christ are firmly established. The scholion also parallels a passage from Didymus's *Commentary on the Psalms*, which, however, is somewhat fragmented in that the word "desolate" in the final sentence of the following passage begins another section of the commentary: "... Concerning which it is said, 'The pillars of heaven lie prostrate, having been carried on heavenly wings.' ... And it is written concerning every reputable person of

22.

Revelation 3.12b–14a: *"And he shall not go out anymore, and I shall write upon him the name of my God and the name of the city of my God, the new Jerusalem, which descends from heaven from my God, and [I shall write upon him] my new name. (13) He who has ears, let him hear what the Spirit says to the churches. (14b) And to the angel of the church in Laodicea, write:"*

The Savior is "*faithful and true*"[89] not because he partakes in faith and truth, but because he is, in essence, firm and true. For being the truth and being *true* are the same with regard to him.[90] Because "*faithful*" is equal to "firm" and "immutable," the Apostle says, "If we are unfaithful, he himself remains faithful, for he is unable to deny himself."[91] And Moses [says], "God is faithful and is not unjust."[92] Regarding this, accept what was written to Timothy, "This is a faithful word,"[93] which is equal to something that always remains and does not fall. And [Scripture] has said, "*He is the faithful and true witness*,"[94] to [affirm] his position of immovability, as he is the *Amen*. Now [Scripture] said that he is "*an archon*[95] *of creation*," not that he is the first creature[96] as the *beginning of creation* itself,[97]

---

the Church which Christ has supported in Himself, 'The pillar and foundation of truth.' And so, the Savior established all these pillars in this firm order, who says, 'I will establish my holy house.' 'Desolate,' He speaks of virtue and piety." Didymus, *Fragmenta in Psalmos (e commentario altero)*, Ps 74.4, 7, Fragment 781A–782A (my translation from TLG #2102.021).

89. Rv 3.14b.

90. Cf. Jn 14.6.

91. 2 Tm 2.13.

92. Dt 32.4.

93. 1 Tm 1.15; 3.1; 4.9; 2 Tm 2.11; Ti 3.8.

94. Rv 3.14b.

95. The Greek word ἀρχή can ambiguously mean "beginning" or "origin," or "ruler." For this quotation see Rv 3.14b.

96. κτίσμα. Origen was often accused of claiming that Jesus was a mere κτίσμα, "creature," contrary to this scholion. See *First Principles* 4.4.1, found in George William Butterworth, trans., *Origen on First Principles: Being Koetschau's Text of the De Principiis* (London: Society for the Promotion of Christian Knowledge, 1936), 314, n. 6. Some scholars, however, argue that Origen never labeled Jesus as a "creature," such as Ilaria L. E. Ramelli, "Origen's Anti-Subordinationism and its Heritage in the Nicene and Cappadocian Line," *Vigiliae Christianae* 65:1 (2011): 21–49.

97. Rv 3.14b.

but as the cause of its existence, the Craftsman of such [creatures]. For as *archon* he is the Maker of what is made, that is, the Creator of creation itself and of [other] archons. But to say, *"I shall vomit you out,"*[98] is the same as, "You have become nauseating to me"—as if [he had said] "since you have become loathsome to me regarding[99] many things."[100] For whenever the Lord casts out the memory of someone from himself, he *vomits* such a one out who became *nauseating* to him, and on account of the monstrosity of his treachery and wickedness, he has no room for him in himself.[101]

23.

Revelation 3.14b–20: *"These things says the Amen, the faithful and true witness, the archon*[102] *of the creation of God. (15) I know your works, that you are neither cold nor hot, [but] I wish that you were either cold or hot! (16) So because you are lukewarm and neither cold nor hot, I am about to vomit you from my mouth. (17) Because you say, 'I am rich and have become enriched, and I have need of nothing,' yet you do not know that you are wretched and miserable and poor and blind and naked. (18) I counsel you to buy from me gold refined with fire, so that you might be rich, and [buy] white clothes, so that you might be clothed and the shame of your nakedness may not be revealed, and eye salve so that you might anoint your eyes, so that you might see. (19) Whomever I love, I rebuke and discipline. Be zealous therefore and repent. (20) Behold, I stand at the door and knock. If someone hears my voice and opens the door, even I shall come to him, and I shall dine with him, and he with me."*

We are taught from these divine voices that in every way it is better to be *cold* and lack the fire of the divine Spirit (for this is

---

98. Rv 3.16.
99. I follow the reading of the manuscript here, not that of Tzamalikos.
100. Perhaps from Is 1.14.
101. Didymus closely parallels this passage in his *Commentary on Zechariah* 1.153–154 (TLG #2102.010; FC 111:59–60). This scholion also seems related to Scholion 22 because these two scholia emphasize that both the Church and Christ are firmly established. The scholion also may be related to Scholion 26 because they both discuss the deity of Christ. In this regard the scholion may reflect fourth-century anti-Arian concerns, but such issues were also discussed earlier and later in the Christian era.
102. ἀρχή, or "ruler," "origin."

supra-sensible coldness) than to think that one is appointed over the affairs of God, yet to possess a middling idleness and to be *lukewarm*, which shows a calling[103] towards thoughtlessness in all things; indeed, the apostle also disparages [such] trickery.[104]

### 24.

Revelation 3.21–22: *"He who conquers, I shall give to him to sit with me on my throne, as I also have conquered and have sat with my Father on his throne. (22) He who has ears, let him hear what the Spirit says to the churches."*

Paul agrees with these things, writing, "And he raised us up together and seated us together in the heavenly [realms] in Christ Jesus."[105] For all the apostles, having conquered the principalities and authorities[106] against whom they had a contest, received the prize of victory, to *sit with the Father* upon twelve thrones, so that they might judge the twelve tribes of Israel.[107] And it was spoken by the Father to the Savior, "Sit at my right hand, until I make your enemies a footstool for your feet."[108] Therefore, that some *sit with the Father on his throne* shows that they shall reign with him.[109] For a throne is a symbol of kingship. For [Scripture] says, "God shall give to him the throne of David his father, and he shall reign over the house of Jacob forever."[110]

Indeed,[111] it is possible to understand you when you speak knowledgeable words, because only you are accustomed to knowledge. Likewise, it is not possible to hear your Spirit because only the one who has a spiritual ear, given to him by God, [can do so], according

103. I follow Turner in reading "calling."

104. In his *First Principles* 3.4.3 Origen discusses Rv 3.16, but only parallels this scholion in a vague and general sense.

105. Eph 2.6.

106. Cf. Eph 6.12.

107. Cf. Mt 19.28.

108. Ps 109.1; Mt 22.44; Heb 1.13.

109. Cf. 2 Tm 2.12.

110. Is 9.7; Lk 1.32–33.

111. Harnack and Tzamalikos regard the remainder of this scholion as an additional note by an author other than the one who wrote the first paragraph, but other scholars disagree; see Turner, "The Text of the Newly Discovered Scholia of Origen on the Apocalypse," 394.

to what is said, "He gave to me an ear to hear."[112] For if the irratio-
nal have an organ for a sense of hearing, [then] only the wise have
an ear of understanding according to the Spirit, concerning which
the Savior said in the plural, "Whoever has ears to hear, let him
hear."[113]

25.

Revelation 4.1: *After these things I looked, and behold, an opened door in
heaven, and the first voice, which I heard speaking with me like a trumpet, was
saying, "Come up here, and I will show you what is necessary to be after these
things."*

It is necessary to peruse the God-breathed Scripture more intelligently, so that we may not incur derision from the wise of the
world.[114] For they, having heard that there was *a door opened in heav-
en*, consign it as an impossible thing to be said. For what we shall
speak to them are not the things that are recorded obviously, but
according to what is hidden. The essence of supra-sensible things
is often signified in Scripture with the title of "*heaven*." Therefore,
whenever it says that *a door was opened in heaven*, we understand it
according to [our] interpretation as the nature of supra-sensible
things, and particularly so whenever one of the saints says that he
ascended there.[115] Notice that it is not written that another [entity]
took John up, like [that which happened to] Elijah, but that he was
appointed to ascend by a voluntary impulse to there where he who
called [him] exists. And he was in *heaven*. But he says that he who
summoned [him did so] with a great *voice* like a *trumpet*, speaking
to him with [the text that] has been presented. But what is spoken
in this manner symbolizes the lofty utterances of supra-sensible
things, which were lucidly presented to him.[116]

---

112. Is 50.4.

113. Mt 11.15, though this injunction actually is in the singular.

114. 1 Cor 1.20.

115. I follow Turner by ignoring the short phrase τὰς πιστώσεις at the end of
this sentence because it makes little sense here and seems simply to be copied from
the next word.

116. Origen loosely parallels this scholion in his *Commentary on John* 2.46–47
(which is adjacent to a passage paralleled by Scholion 3).

## 26.

Revelation 4.2–11: *Immediately I was in the Spirit, and behold, a throne was set in heaven, and upon the throne was one who sat.* (3) *And he who sat was in appearance like a jasper and sardis stone, and a rainbow encircled the throne, which was in appearance like emerald.* (4) *Around the throne were twenty-four thrones, and upon the thrones were sitting twenty-four elders, who were enrobed in white garments, and upon their heads were golden crowns.* (5) *And from the throne issued flashes of lightning and sounds and peals of thunder. And seven lamps of fire burned before his throne, and they are the seven spirits of God.* (6) *And before the throne there was [something] like a glassy sea, like crystal. And in the midst of the throne and around the throne were four creatures, full of eyes on the front and back.* (7) *And the first creature was like a lion, and the second creature was like a calf, and the third creature had the face of a man, and the fourth creature was like a flying eagle.* (8) *And as for the four creatures, each one had upon it six wings, and they were full of eyes around the inside and outside, and they did not have rest day or night, saying, "Holy, Holy, Holy Lord God Almighty, who was and who is and who is coming."* (9) *And whenever the creatures would give glory and honor and thanksgiving to him who sits upon the throne, to him who lives forever and ever, amen,* (10) *the twenty-four elders would fall before him who sits upon the throne and worship him who lives forever and ever and cast their crowns before the throne, saying,* (11) *"Worthy are you, our Lord and God, the Holy One, to receive glory and honor and power, because you have created all things and through your will they exist and were created."*

This is the one who was not created, but the one who *created*. But rational beings, after they came to exist and to be, accepted being created. For, "He spoke," says [Scripture], "and they came to be; he commanded, and they were created."[117] Indeed, one is created for good works for this [purpose]: to be the workmanship of God with a pure heart.[118] And "did not this very Father himself create you and make you and fashion you?"[119] It must be noted

117. Ps 32.9; 148.5.
118. Cf. Eph 2.10.
119. Dt 32.6. After this quotation Tzamalikos conjecturally inserts an entire sentence, which I have omitted. For a critique of Tzamalikos's conjecture, see Darius Müller and Edmund Gerke, "Eine deutsche Übersetzung der Scholia in Apocalypsin mit Einleitung," in *Studien zum Text der Apokalypse II*, ed. Marcus Sigismund

that [Scripture] also says that *creatures* exist by the *will* of God. For this reason,[120] the existence of the Savior was not dependent upon the will of the Father. For he is not a *creature*. Indeed, the following [section] clearly indicates this.[121]

27.

Revelation 5.1–5: *And I saw at the right hand and in the midst of him who sat upon the throne, a scroll written on the inside and the outside, sealed with seven seals. (2) And I saw a strong angel preaching in a great voice, "Who is worthy to open the scroll and loose its seals?" (3) And no one was able in heaven above, nor upon the earth, nor below the earth, to open the scroll or to look at it. (4) And I wept greatly because no one was found worthy to open the scroll or to look at it. (5) And one from the elders says to me, "Do not weep. Behold, the lion has conquered, he who is from the tribe of Judah, the root of David, who opens the scroll and its seven seals."*

Someone shall say concerning this *scroll* that it is every aspect of foreknowledge from which judgment from God is brought upon men, both pleasant and unpleasant. And since the scroll not only encompasses things concerning physical matters, but also supra-sensible things, *it is written inside and outside*. And since "the judgments and ways of God are unsearchable,"[122] then accordingly, as he reaches throughout the whole universe and judges and bestows [verdicts] on each [person], the *scroll* is *sealed* with a divine number of *seals*. But when the time arrives in which it is necessary to gather those upon the earth, some to pleasantness, but some to gloom, one is sought who has such power that he may take the *scroll* from the *right hand* of Him who holds it and may *loose its seals*. Then, it is clear from the following that no one who has come to exist, neither a heavenly nor an earthly [being], is *found worthy*—due to the

---

and Darius Müller, Arbeiten zur neutestamentlichen Textforschung 50 (Berlin: De Gruyter, 2017), 436; https://doi.org/10.1515/9783110558784.

120. Tzamalikos notes that the only Christian author to use the construction ὅθεν οὐκ + adjective is Didymus; see Tzamalikos, *An Ancient Commentary*, 147.

121. The scholion may reflect fourth-century anti-Arian concerns, but such issues were also discussed earlier and later in the Christian era. This scholion appears related to Scholion 22 in that they both discuss the deity of Christ.

122. Rom 11.33.

inferiority of [their] nature—to reveal this word of foreknowledge through judgment and administration, [but] only he who is from the seed of David according to the flesh[123] appeared *worthy* to do that which is contained in the *scroll*. For the Father judges no one.[124] This one appeared *who is the lion from the tribe of Judah, the root of David*, the *Lamb who was slaughtered*.[125] Moses wrote concerning this *scroll* and in Isaiah it is written concerning it as well, as in many other parts of Scripture. Since before [his] advent the first covenant had great obscurity, since *what was written was sealed with seven seals*. But thus it became clear after the resurrection of the Lord that those who endured with effort the opening [of the *scroll*] speak concerning the *slaughtered Lamb*, "Were not our hearts burning in us, when he explained to us the Scriptures?"[126]

### 28.

Revelation 5.6–8a: *And I saw, in the midst of the throne and of the four creatures and in the midst of the elders, a Lamb standing as though he were slaughtered, having seven horns and seven eyes, which are the seven spirits of God sent into all the earth. (7) And he came and took [the scroll] from the right hand of him who sat upon the throne. (8a) And when he took the scroll ...*

"After I recognized," [Scripture] says, "*that the root of David, he who conquered, the lion from the tribe of Judah, had taken the scroll in order to loose its seals, I saw, in the midst of the throne*[127] *and of the four creatures and of the elders, a Lamb standing as though he were slaughtered*."[128] For after the Resurrection and Ascension, the *Lamb* was seen not slaughtered anymore, but he was seen *as though he were slaughtered* and still *standing*,[129]

123. Cf. Rom 1.3.

124. Cf. Jn 5.22.

125. Rv 5.12.

126. Lk 24.32. Origen parallels content in this scholion in his *Commentary on the Psalms* 1.1 (PG 12:1077) and his *Homilies on Exodus* 12.4 (also paralleled by Scholion 20). This scholion also parallels Scholion 20 directly because they both draw upon the account in Lk 24 to make the same theological point.

127. The manuscript here reads "in the midst of heaven," but Turner and Tzamalikos both suspect that the original reading was "throne."

128. Rv 5.5–6.

129. I follow Turner here instead of Tzamalikos.

that is to say, no longer subject to change. And so, if in his new state he has *seven horns*, then he possesses a holy and blessed kingdom, for *the spirits* are a symbol of this. Besides the *seven horns* he also has *seven eyes*. These are none other than the *seven spirits of God, which go forth upon the earth* overseeing the practices of men. This agrees with the following: "The eyes of the Lord are seven, which look over all the earth."[130]

29.

Revelation 5.8b–6.2: ... *the four creatures and the twenty-four elders fell before the Lamb, each having a harp and golden bowls full of incense, which are the prayers of the saints.* (9) *And they sang a new song, saying, "Worthy are you to take the scroll and to open its seals, because you were slaughtered and you purchased us for God by your blood from every tribe and tongue and people and nation,* (10) *and you have made them to be our kings and priests for God, and they shall reign upon the earth."* (11) *And I looked, and I heard a sound of many angels around the throne, the creatures and the elders, and the number of them was a thousand times a thousand and ten thousand times ten thousand,*[131](12) *who were speaking in a great voice: "Worthy is the Lamb who was slaughtered, to receive power and wealth and wisdom and strength and honor and glory and blessing."* (13) *And all creation, which was in heaven and on earth and under the earth and on the sea, and whatever is, and all the things in them, I heard them saying, "To him who sits upon the throne and to the Lamb be blessing and honor and glory and power for ever and ever."* (14) *And the four creatures said, "Amen," and the elders fell and worshiped.*

(6.1) *And I saw that the Lamb opened one of the seven seals, and I heard*

130. Zec 4.10. Tzamalikos (*An Ancient Commentary*, 329) notes that the phrase μετὰ τὸ ἐγνωκέναι, "after I recognized," occurs in this exact form only in Origen, *Exhortation to Martyrdom* 32.11. Similar notions about the number seven being "holy and blessed" are found in Didymus, who even quotes from the same passage of Zechariah as this scholion when he discusses the subject. See his *Commentarii in Psalmos* 22–26.10, page 107, lines 22–25 (TLG #2102.017): "For it is often shown to us that seven always is blessed. For 'God blessed the seventh day and made it holy,' and, 'the eyes of the Lord, which look over all the earth, are seven'" (my translation from Gronewald 1968). Scholion 9 also makes a similar claim about the number seven.

131. Literally: "ten thousands times ten thousands and thousands times thousands."

*one of the four creatures saying as with a voice of thunder, "Come." (2) And behold, a white horse! And he who sat upon it had a bow, and a crown was given to him, and he came conquering and in order to conquer.*

Somewhere it is said, "Let my prayer be directed as incense before you."[132] *Bowls full* of these *incenses* are the guides of those who genuinely pray to Christ. And one could say that the *harps* are their power, which is melodiously and gracefully tuned, by which they know and love Christ. But why, in *singing a new song*, do they say, *"You are worthy,* O Master, Savior, *to take the scroll,"* etc.? Now these things plainly concern him who was crucified, who was led as a sheep to slaughter.[133] Regarding the way in which he was slaughtered, the flowing blood was given as the price on behalf of those who are saved. And since he was crucified not on behalf of a portion or [on behalf] of one *nation* of men, he *purchased by his blood* [some] from *every tribe* of Israel and *every language* of men and indeed of [every] *people.*

Moreover, it is [possible] to take a different [meaning] for both *"people"* and *"nation,"* by saying that those taken from *"people"* are from the pure and wise men, but those *purchased* from *"the nation"* are from the commoners and crowds. This preferable hypothesis confirms the number of the *twenty-four elders* from the passage at hand. For these confess that they were *"purchased from men"* and were chosen.

And so we who have read these things and have learned both that *incense is the prayers of the saints*[134] and that spiritual sacrifices and good works are pleasing to God,[135] we see that from the first advent of Christ, "In every place incense and a pure sacrifice are offered in the name of the Lord. For his name is great among the nations,"[136] on account of the teaching of Christ, as the prophet says.[137]

---

132. Ps 140.2.
133. Cf. Is 53.7.
134. Cf. Rv 5.8b.
135. Cf. 1 Pt 2.5.
136. Mal 1.11.
137. Origen in *Against Celsus* 8.17 quotes from Rv 5.8 and juxtaposes it with Ps 140.2, just as this scholion does.

30.

Revelation 6.3–8: *And when he opened the second seal, I heard the second creature saying, "Come!" (4) And another fiery horse came out. And to him who sat upon it, there was given to him to take peace from the earth so that [men] might kill one another. And a great sword was given to him. (5) And when he opened the third seal, I heard the third creature saying, "Come!" And behold, a black horse! And he who sat upon it had a scale in his hand. (6) And I heard [something] like a voice in the midst of the four creatures saying, "A quart of wheat for a denarius, and three quarts of barley for a denarius. And the oil and the wine do not harm." (7) And when he opened the fourth seal, I heard the fourth creature saying, "Come!" (8) And behold a pale horse! And as for him who sat upon it, death was his name, and Hades followed him. And authority was given to him over the four [corners] of the earth, to kill with sword and with famine and with death and by the beasts of the earth.*

From the Scriptures it is [possible] to find that some holy faculties are like God's body, such as his hands, which minister, and his eyes, which are capable of sight, and his ears, which marshal prayers, and his feet,[138] which by God's providence drive away those who live upon the earth.[139] And so since [Scripture] is about to mention the great *wrath of God*,[140] it is not undirected passion that is called the *"wrath of God,"* for that does not belong to him, but [*wrath*] is appointed as a necessity for those who are in need of it, to which [*wrath*] they are also handed over as unworthy of God, so that they might long for God, whom they currently despise because they are under the authority of one who is worse [than they]. And the devil is the *wrath of God*.[141]

For in Second Kingdoms it is even said, "And he caused the wrath of the Lord to move against Israel, and he aroused David,

138. I follow Turner's reading here. Tzamalikos makes a conjecture here, and on the basis of his conjecture finds a parallel with Didymus; see Tzamalikos, *An Ancient Commentary*, 343.

139. These ideas are similar to thoughts behind Origen's *Commentary on John* 1.281–282 and *Homilies on Genesis* 1.13, the latter of which parallels material found in Scholion 15.

140. Rv 6.17.

141. Regarding "the wrath of God" Tzamalikos notes very similar parallels with authors like Origen, Basil of Caesarea, Theodoret, and especially Didymus; see Tzamalikos, *An Ancient Commentary*, 341–42, 347.

saying, 'Go and count Israel and Judah.'"[142] And the *wrath of God* "which aroused David" is [grammatically feminine], yet [the feminine form of the word] "saying" [is not in the text]; rather, it is [the masculine] "saying."[143] So then, aside from God himself, who told a certain person to speak many things to the saints, his wrath is a certain other being. And this being says these things and commands sin [and] to sin. After which, punishment from God follows upon those who obeyed this kind of wrath that has been mentioned.

But how can [that wrath], which punishes, even justly punishes, [people] for sin, [then] incite them to sin, so that after persuading them to sin it might justly punish?[144] For then the cause of sin would unjustly punish the sinner. But just as has been said, the *wrath of God* is the devil, who persuades people to sin, wishing to take under his command the sinner because he has sinned.

For also in First Chronicles this same cause is related concerning David. [Scripture] speaks in the following way: "And the devil stood in Israel and aroused David to count Israel."[145] Now [the phrase] "he aroused" is the term used in both Second Kingdoms and First Chronicles, the former about the "wrath of the Lord," and the latter about the "devil." But if the one who aroused is the cause of sin, and if the devil is the cause of sin, then the devil is named by both terms—the one through a common expression and the other, which has escaped the notice of many, is named "the wrath of the Lord"—according to which the Great Song elsewhere says, "You have sent forth your wrath, and it consumed them as straw," etc.[146]

For anything that is sent by someone is different from the one

142. 2 Sm 24.1. (In the Greek tradition 1 and 2 Samuel are called 1 and 2 Kingdoms.)

143. The author here is making a grammatical argument, which is unclear in English translation. He argues that in the passage at hand it cannot be the wrath of God that aroused David because the Greek word for "wrath" is feminine and the participle that is used for "arouse" and "say" is masculine, thus implying that it must be someone or something other than the wrath of God. This argument depends on the Greek translation of the Septuagint. It does not, however, hold up in the Hebrew because the particular Hebrew words חרה and אמר are infinitives and therefore do not have gender.

144. I am indebted to the suggestions of Turner for the translation of this last sentence.

145. 1 Chr 21.1.

146. Ex 15.7.

who sent it. Therefore, who would be sent as wrath against the Egyptians except, as we have learned from First Chronicles, the devil? Hence if sinners are said to be handed over to the *wrath of God*, one must understand that they are handed over to the devil, as also Paul [said to the church in] Corinth, "whom you shall hand over to Satan so that they may be taught not to blaspheme."[147]

We[148] also have overseeing angels who even help us [in our] good deeds, and a universal judgment is before them all, as [Scripture] says, "Arise, be judged before the mountains; let the hills hear your voice. Hear, O hills, the judgment of the Lord."[149] It also seems from these [notions] that the word of God ordained that the affairs of men will be judged along with the powers who have been entrusted [with them], so that [at that time] one might be able to demonstrate if he was found in sin or blame because of some neglect or omission of the [angels'] undertakings on behalf of men. We can understand this by providing an example. Come, tell of a lawsuit concerning people with bishops, and a lawsuit of sons with a father, and a lawsuit of students with a teacher. Then, at that time, people will demonstrate the cause of their sinning to be from their bishops. But sometimes the bishop might show all that he has done himself and that he did not omit any of the things becoming of a zealous ruler and shall demonstrate that the people are liable for [their] crimes. In the same way consider[150] also sons who accuse fathers regarding [their] education, and they defend themselves by showing that their fathers are the cause of such errors. But in contrast fathers might make a defense that they did not neglect an education that accords with the word of God for [their] sons, but reproved their sons because of their own laziness when they were found in sin. It is not out of place from these things to consider also disciples and [their] teachers.[151]

147. 1 Cor 5.5. Origen makes very similar arguments in *Against Celsus* 4.72 and his *Commentary on Romans* 1.16.3.

148. Harnack regards the following paragraph as being added by the scholiast, but Turner and Tzamalikos disagree.

149. Mi 6.1–2.

150. According to Tzamalikos no author before the tenth century makes use of the idiom τὸ δὲ ὅμοιον νόει, "in the same way consider," in any form except for Origen, who uses it three times; see Tzamalikos, *An Ancient Commentary*, 356.

151. This last paragraph is strikingly similar to the argument that Origen makes

31.

Revelation 6.9–7.8: *And when he opened the fifth seal, I saw beneath the altar the souls of those who have been slaughtered on account of the word of God and on account of the testimony to the Lamb that they bore. (10) And they cried out in a great voice, saying, "How long, O Master, holy and true, will you not judge and avenge our blood upon those who dwell upon the earth?" (11) And a white robe was given to them, and they were told to rest a little, until their fellow slaves might also be fulfilled and their brothers who are also about to be killed as they themselves [were]. (12) And I saw that he opened the sixth seal, and a great earthquake occurred, and the sun was dark, and it became like sackcloth, and the whole moon became like blood. (13) And the stars of heaven fell upon the earth as a fig tree casts its leaves when it is shaken by a great wind. (14) And heaven was opened like a rolled-up scroll, and every mountain and every island was shaken from its place. (15) And the kings of the earth and the magistrates and chiliarchs and the rich and the strong and every slave and freedman hid themselves in caves and among the rocks of the mountains. (16) And they say to the mountains and the rocks, "Fall upon us and hide us from the face of him who sits upon the throne and from the wrath of the Lamb. (17) The great day of his wrath has come, and who is able to stand?"*

*(7.1) After this I saw four angels standing on the four corners of the earth, restraining the four winds of the earth, so that the wind would not blow on the earth nor upon the sea nor upon any tree. (2) And I saw another angel ascending from the eastern sun, having seals of the living God, and he shouted in a great voice to the four angels to whom it was given to harm the earth and the sea, (3) saying, "Do not harm the earth and the sea nor the trees until we have sealed the slaves of our God upon their foreheads. (4) And I heard the number of those who were sealed; one hundred forty-four thousand were sealed from all the tribes of the sons of Israel. (5) From the tribe of Judah twelve thousand were sealed, from the tribe of Reuben twelve thousand, from the tribe of Gad twelve thousand, (6) from the tribe of Naphtali twelve thousand, from the tribe of Manasseh twelve thousand, (7) from the tribe of Simeon twelve thousand, from the tribe of Levi twelve thousand, from the tribe of Issachar twelve thousand, (8) from the tribe of Zebulon twelve thousand, from the tribe of Joseph twelve thousand, from the tribe of Benjamin twelve thousand were sealed.*

---

in his *Homilies on Luke* 13.4–6, the same passage that is paralleled in Scholia 6 and 12. See also Origen's *Homilies on Numbers* 20.3.6–7; 20.4.2; 14.2.9; and 11.4.5 for similar if not identical arguments.

Because grievous things are about to happen, a certain minis-
tering angel of God calls to those who have been entrusted with
the labors[152] not to begin them *until the slaves of God have received seals
upon [their] foreheads.* The same thing is commanded with different
words in Ezekiel the prophet, "Kill, do not spare anyone, but for
those who have the sign, do not approach."[153] And so since they
who were punished suffer this on account of their own sins, a certain mark, which signifies the accompaniment of righteousness, is
set upon the *forehead* of those who are righteous, that is to say, upon
their bold virtue. They who have the aforementioned sign confess
thanks to him who gave it, saying, "The light of your face is a sign
upon us, O Lord,"[154] and again, "You have given those who fear
you signs to flee from the bow of your face."[155]

One[156] must ask if, while John was still in this life, it was possible
that there were so many *thousands* of male *virgins* from Israel according to the flesh.[157] Since indeed a physical interpretation brings a
great impossibility—yet the things which are in the holy book are
true—so it is necessary to receive what has been set forth [in the
text] according to the spiritual formula. For it follows that the true
Israel, which has no deceit,[158] was divided into tribes. And so were
we to say that there was so great a multitude of male *virgins* from
this [spiritual] Israel, we would not say what is impossible, for everyone, both Jews and Greeks, who came to Christ, fulfilled this
supra-sensible nation. And since the [spiritual] Hebrews in this way
have great harmony and accord, they live with each other by being
fashioned in one mind and one thought,[159] and are also equal to
so great a number, [for] they are allocated by its divisions. Indeed,
the number is a square of the same, being squared from twelve.

---

152. τοὺς ἐγχειρισθέντας τὰ ἐπίπονα, "those who have been entrusted with the
labors": identical vocabulary in a slightly different form is used only by Didymus;
see Tzamalikos, *An Ancient Commentary*, 360.

153. Ezek 9.5–6.

154. Ps 4.7.

155. Ps 59.6.

156. Harnack regards the following paragraph as coming from a later scholiast,
but Turner and Tzamalikos disagree.

157. Cf. 1 Cor 10.18.

158. Cf. Jn 1.47.

159. Cf. 1 Cor 1.10.

For twelve times twelve is one hundred forty-four. And the square figure is a symbol of steadfast stature.[160]

## 32.

Revelation 7.9a: *After these things I looked, and behold, a great crowd which no one was able to number, from every nation and tribe and people and tongue, standing before the throne and before the Lamb* ...

Further down[161] it says that these *one hundred forty-four thousand* are *virgins*.[162] And if you were to accept that these *tribes* refer to those who are said to be physically in *Israel*, where might you find a *virgin* in each tribe, [especially] twelve thousand virgins? But we do find this in the Church, since the Word teaches [us] to be zealous for virginity, not according to a command,[163] nor so that a noose might be imposed upon those who listen,[164] but voluntarily in cheer and gladness. Just as it is written, *"And so these are they who have not been defiled with women,"* as has been said, *"For they are virgins. And a lie was not found in their mouth."*[165]

## 33.

Revelation 7.9b–13a: ... *clothed in white robes and palms were in their hands, (10) and they cried in a great voice saying, "Salvation be to our God, who sits upon the throne, and to the Lamb." (11) And all the angels stood in a circle around the throne and [around] the elders and the four creatures, and they fell before the throne on their faces and worshiped God, (12) saying, "Amen.*

160. This scholion seems to be linked with Scholion 32 and is quite similar to Origen's *Commentary on John* 1.4–8. Didymus also parallels the scholion in his *Commentary on Zechariah* 3.67–73 (TLG #2102.010, trans. Hill, 200–201). Tzamalikos notes that Didymus uses squared numbers elsewhere in his exegesis; see Tzamalikos, *An Ancient Commentary*, 369.

161. This phrase suggests that this particular scholion comes from a work specifically on the Apocalypse and is not merely an incidental comment.

162. Rv 14.4.

163. Cf. 1 Cor 7.6; 2 Cor 8.8.

164. 1 Cor 7.35.

165. Rv 14.4–5. Origen remarkably parallels content in this scholion in his *Homilies on Exodus* 1.2 and *Commentary on John* 1.4–8. The content of this scholion overlaps with Scholion 31, likely because they deal with the same subject matter.

*Blessing and glory and wisdom and thanksgiving and honor and power and strength be to our God for ever and ever. Amen." (13a) And one from the elders answered, saying to me . . .*

These *white robes* are able to show their immaculate intentions and deeds. In addition to the *white robes* in which they are *clothed*, they hold *palms* in their *hands*, a symbol of victory, by which they conquered the world.[166] *"These are they who come out of the great persecution,"*[167] through martyrdom and confession, and it is clear that [they come] through other adversities on account of Christ, which both evil men and demons bring against the disciples of Jesus. *"Having washed and made white the robes,"* which clothe [them], *"in the blood of the Lamb,"* who was slaughtered on their behalf.[168] But so that we men might consider the constancy of their worship,[169] the time is named according to our reckoning by dividing it into *day and night.*[170]

### 34.

Revelation 7.13b–9.19: . . . *"Who are these who are clothed in white robes and from where have they come?" (14) And I said to him, "My Lord, you know." And he said to me, "These are those who came from the great persecution and washed their robes and whitened them in the blood of the Lamb. (15) On account of this they are before the throne of God and worship him day and night in his temple. And he who sits upon the throne shall dwell among them. (16) They shall not hunger anymore, nor shall they thirst anymore, nor shall the sun fall upon them, nor any heat, (17) because the Lamb who is above the midst of the throne shall shepherd them and guide them to living springs of water, and God shall wipe away every tear from their eyes."*

*(8.1) And when he opened the seventh seal, there was silence in heaven for about half an hour. (2) And I saw the seven angels who stood before God, and seven trumpets were given to them. (3) And another angel came and stood before the altar, having a golden censer, and much incense was given to him so that he*

---

166. Cf. Jn 16.33. Harnack regards the rest of the scholion as coming from a later scholiast, but Turner and Tzamalikos disagree.

167. Rv 7.14.

168. Ibid.

169. Tzamalikos notes that phraseology in this scholion is used only by Philo of Alexandria; see Tzamalikos, *An Ancient Commentary*, 382.

170. Rv 7.15.

*might offer the prayers of all the saints upon the golden altar that is before the throne. (4) And the smoke of the incense from the hand of the angel arose before God with the prayers of the saints. (5) And the angel took the censer and filled it from the fire of the altar and cast it upon the earth. And there were peals of thunder and noises and flashes of lightning and earthquakes. (6) And the seven angels who had the seven trumpets readied themselves so that they might sound [them]. (7) And the first [angel] sounded a trumpet, and there were hail and fire mixed in blood, and they were thrown to the earth. And a third of the earth was burned, and a third of the trees were burned, and all the green grass was burned. (8) And the second angel sounded a trumpet, and [something] like a great mountain that was burning with fire was cast into the sea, and the third of the sea became blood. (9) And a third of the creatures that are in the sea died, those that have life, and a third of the ships were destroyed. (10) And the third angel sounded a trumpet, and a great star fell from heaven burning like a lamp. And it fell upon the third of the rivers and upon the springs of waters. (11) And the name of the star was called Wormwood. And a third of the waters became as wormwood, and many of the men died from the waters because they were made bitter. (12) And the fourth angel sounded a trumpet, and a third of the sun was struck, and a third of the moon, and a third of the stars, so that a third of them were darkened, and a third of the day did not shine,[171] and the night similarly. (13) And I saw, and I heard one eagle flying in the midst of heaven, saying in a great voice, "Woe, woe, woe to those who dwell upon the earth on account of the remaining sounds of the trumpets that the three angels are about to trumpet.*

*(9.1) And the fifth angel sounded a trumpet, and I saw a star that had fallen from heaven to the earth, and the key of the shaft of the abyss was given to him. (2) And he opened the shaft of the abyss, and smoke ascended from the shaft like smoke from a burning furnace. And the sun and the air were darkened from the smoke of the shaft. (3) And from the smoke came locusts upon the earth, and authority was given to them as scorpions have authority on the earth. (4) And it was told to them that they should not harm the grass of the earth nor any green thing nor any tree, except the men who did not have the seal of God upon their foreheads. (5) And it was given to them so that they might not kill them, but so that they might torment them for five months. And the torment of them was like the torment of a scorpion when it strikes a man. (6) And in those days men shall seek death, and they shall not find it; they will long to die, and death shall flee from them. (7) And the likeness of the locusts*

---

171. There is an error of repetition in the manuscript here: "and as for the day, a third of it did not shine, and as for the day, a third of it did not shine."

*was like horses ready for war, and the likeness of what was upon their heads was like golden crowns,*[172] *and their faces were like the faces of men, (8) and they had [hair] like the hair of women, and their teeth were like those of lions. (9) And they had breastplates like breastplates of iron, and the sound of their wings was like the sound of many chariots of horses rushing to war. (10) And they had tails like scorpions and stings, and in their tails also their authority was to harm man for five months. (11) And they have a king over them, the angel of the abyss. The name for him in Hebrew is "Abbadon," but in Greek he has the name "Apollyon." (12) The first woe has passed. Behold, two more woes are still to come after these things. (13) And the sixth angel sounded a trumpet, and I heard one voice from the four horns of the altar of gold that is before God, (14) saying to the sixth angel, who had the trumpet, "Loose the four angels who are bound at the great river Euphrates." (15) And the four angels were released who are ready for [that] hour and day and month and year, so that they might kill a third of men. (16) And the number of the soldiers of the horsemen was twenty thousand times ten thousand. I heard their number. (17) And in this manner, I saw the horsemen in the vision, and they sat upon [their horses], which had fiery, hyacinth, and sulfurous breastplates. And the heads of the horses were like the heads of lions, and from their mouths poured forth fire and smoke and brimstone. (18) From these plagues they killed a third of men, also from the fire and smoke and brimstone that poured forth from their mouths. (19) For the power of the horses is in their mouth and in their tails. For their tails are like serpents, which have heads, and by them they do harm.*

Consider if it is possible that the *washed and whitened robes* of those who went up from the *great persecution* are their bodies, now being seen resurrected beforehand as incorruptible and spiritual.[173]

### 35.

Revelation 9.20–10.3a: *And the rest of men who were not killed by these plagues, who did not repent from the works of their hands, so that they would stop worshiping demons and golden and silver and bronze and stone and wooden idols, which are not able to see nor able to hear or walk. (21) And they did not repent from their murders nor from their sorceries nor from their sexual immorality nor from their thefts.*

172. Literally: "golden crowns like gold."
173. Cf. 1 Cor 15.44, 52.

(10.1) *And I saw another strong angel descending from heaven, who was clothed with a cloud, and a rainbow was upon his head, and his face was like the sun, and his feet were like pillars of fire.* (2) *And he had in his hand a little opened scroll. And he set his right foot upon the sea, and his left upon the earth,* (3) *and he cried in a great voice as when a lion roars.*

God, having decided to subject sinners to *plagues*, permitted some men to go without the trials of *these plagues*, [yet] they still continued in what they were doing. And as many as did not taste [the former plagues], two plagues[174] were [still] left, so that they might have a place of *repentance* in order that they might not still *worship the golden demons* and the other materials from which statues are constructed. This shows that some *worship golden demons and silver and bronze and also wooden [demons]*, so that [these] demons should be understood as spirits who watch over the soulless images. "*Golden ...*" and the rest [of the idols], which have no sense of sight or hearing nor do they walk, are physical statues. For, "They have mouths and do not talk," etc.,[175] as is written in the Psalms.

## 36.

Revelation 10.3b–11.18a: *And when he cried, the seven thunders spoke [with] their voices,* (4) *and when the seven thunders spoke, I was about to write, and I heard a voice from heaven, saying, "Seal what the seven thunders spoke, and do not write them."* (5) *And the angel, whom I saw standing on the sea and on the earth, raised his right hand to heaven* (6) *and swore by him who lives forever and ever, who created the heaven and the things in it and the earth and the things in it and the sea and the things in it, that there may be no more delay,*[176] (7) *but in the days of the voice of the seventh angel, when he is about to trumpet, [then] the mystery of God is also completed, as he has proclaimed [it] to his slaves the prophets.* (8) *And the voice that I heard from heaven was speaking again with me and saying, "Go, take the little open scroll that is in the hand of the angel who stands on the sea and on the earth."* (9) *And I went to the angel, saying to him, "Give to me the little scroll." And he says to me, "Take and eat it, and it will make your heart bitter, but in your mouth it shall*

---

174. I follow Turner here instead of Tzamalikos.
175. Ps 134.16.
176. Literally: "so that time might no longer be."

*be sweet as honey." (10) And I took the little scroll from the hand of the angel and ate it, and in my mouth it was sweet as honey. And when I had eaten it, my heart was made bitter. (11) And they said to me,*[177] *"It is necessary for you to prophesy again to peoples and nations and tongues and many kings."*

*(11.1) And a reed like a staff was given to me, and the angel stood, saying, "Arise and measure the temple of God and the altar and those who worship in it, (2) and leave out the court that is outside the temple and do not measure it, because it is given to the nations, and they shall trample the holy city forty-two months. (3) And I shall give to my two witnesses, and they shall prophesy for one thousand two hundred sixty days clothed in sackcloth. (4) These are the two olive trees and the two lampstands that stand before the Lord of the earth. (5) And if anyone wishes to harm them, fire shall pour from their mouths and shall consume their enemies. And if anyone wishes to harm them, it is necessary that in this way he shall be killed. (6) These have authority even to shut heaven, so that no rain shall rain in the days of their prophecy. And they have authority over the waters to turn them to blood and to strike the earth with every plague as often as they will. (7) [And whenever they finish] their testimony, the beast that ascends from the abyss shall make war with them and shall conquer them and shall kill them. (8) And their corpses shall be on the street of the great city, which is spiritually called Sodom and Egypt, where also their Lord was crucified. (9) And they who are from the peoples and tribes and tongues and nations shall see their corpses for three-and-a-half days, and their corpses shall not be allowed to be placed in tombs. (10) And those who dwell upon the earth shall rejoice over them and shall be glad and shall send gifts to one another because these two prophets tormented those who dwell upon the earth. (11) And after three-and-a-half days a spirit of life from God entered into them, and they stood upon their feet, and great fear fell upon all those who saw them. (12) And I heard a great voice from heaven, saying to them, "Come up here." And they ascended into heaven on a cloud, and their enemies saw them. (13) And in that hour there was a great earthquake, and a tenth of the city fell, and seven thousand names of men were killed in the earthquake, and the rest became afraid. And they gave glory to the God of heaven. (14) The second woe is past. Behold, the third woe is coming quickly. (15) And the seventh angel sounded a trumpet, and there were great voices in heaven, saying, "The kingdom of this world*[178] *has become that of our God and of his Christ, and he shall reign forever and ever." (16) And the twenty-four elders who were before the throne of God, who were sitting upon their thrones,*

177. Literally: "and they say to me."
178. Literally: "of his world."

*fell upon their faces and worshiped God,* (17) *saying, "We give thanks to you, Lord God Almighty, who is and who was, because you have taken your great power and have reigned,* (18a) *and the nations were enraged."*

Great words are explained to the righteous as being *thunders*. And the prophet perhaps makes this clear, saying, "A voice of your thunder was in the wheel."[179] For if you look there, at a wheel, as you see the wheel rotate,[180] there you will perceive thunder. And also when you examine the things concerning the sons of thunder, James and John, whom Jesus called, "Boanerges, that is, 'sons of thunder,'"[181] you will find that in all likelihood they are called the "sons of thunder" on account of the lofty utterings of their thoughts and teachings.[182]

*"For I heard,"*[183] he says, *"seven thunders, and as much as the seven thunders said, I was about to write. And it was told to me, 'Do not write as much as the seven thunders said.'"*[184] So you understand that at these events such *thunders spoke* words that can be written, yet were not written, and that the holy John heard an articulate *voice* through such a sound. But perhaps, if you were to attend to Scripture, you would find that the *seven thunders* that *spoke* to John are namely: one thunder, wisdom; the other thunder, understanding; the third thunder, counsel; the fourth thunder, strength; the fifth thunder, knowledge; the sixth thunder, piety;[185] the seventh thunder, fear.[186] If I were to hear *thunders speaking* these things, I would not[187] be able to write

179. Or "whirlwind." Ps 76.19.

180. I follow Turner over Tzamalikos here.

181. Mk 3.17.

182. This passage is vaguely similar to Origen's *Homilies on Genesis* 1.13, which is also paralleled in Scholia 15 and 30.

183. Harnack regards the following paragraph as coming from a later scholiast, but Tzamalikos disagrees.

184. Rv 10.3–4.

185. The manuscript reads "understanding," which has already been used for the second thunder.

186. Cf. Is 11.2. An impressive parallel can be found between this scholion and Origen's *Homilies on the Psalms*, Ps. 76 hom. 4.2–3, where Origen also speaks of a wheel with thunder in it and correlates it to the seven thunders of Revelation and to Is 11.2 as well as to the fact that John and James were called the Sons of Thunder.

187. I follow Turner here, who supplies the word "not."

[them], for I do not think that the world itself could hold the books that would be written[188] from the *voice* of the saints speaking *thunders* in Christ Jesus, to whom be glory forever and ever. Amen.[189]

37.

Revelation 11.18b–12.2: (18b) *And your wrath and the time of the dead to be judged came and to reward your slaves the prophets and the saints and those who fear your name, both the small and the great, and to destroy those who destroy the earth.* (19) *And the temple of God was opened, which is in heaven, and the ark of the covenant of the Lord was seen in his temple, and there were flashes of lightning and sounds and peals of thunder and an earthquake and great hail.*

(12.1) *And a great sign was seen in heaven, a woman clothed in the sun, and the moon was beneath her feet, and upon her head was a crown of twelve stars.* (2) *And she had a [child] in [her] womb, [and] she cried, being in pain and agony, to give birth.*

"*And your wrath and the time of the dead came*," according to the *time* of the consummation, when all shall appear before the judgment seat of Christ in order that each shall deservedly receive according to how he has lived.[190] The *wrath* of God is appointed, which each "has treasured for himself in the day of wrath and the revelation of the righteous judgment of God."[191] In which *time* also the *wages of the prophets and saints and of those who fear the name of God* shall be rendered. And so it makes clear that of those who receive wages, there

---

188. Cf. Jn 21.25.

189. "Amen" may indicate that this scholion contains the conclusion of a homily. Origen quotes from Rv 10.4 and compares it with Jn 21.25, as the author of this scholion does, in his *Commentary on John* 5.3; 13.27–28, 33, but he does not correlate the seven thunders to the seven spirits of wisdom. Elsewhere, in *Commentary on John* 1.147, 13.33, and *Homilies on Jeremiah* 8.5.2, Origen does talk about the seven spirits of wisdom, but does not correlate them with the seven thunders of Rv 10.4. Didymus correlates the seven spirits of wisdom with a different passage from the Apocalypse in his *Commentary on Zechariah* 1.278–282 (TLG #2102.010, trans. Hill, 85–86). Didymus also refers in his *Commentary on Zechariah* 1.254 (TLG #2102.010, trans. Hill, 80–81) to the seven spirits of wisdom as they relate to the seven eyes on the stone in Zec 3.9.

190. Cf. 2 Cor 5.10.

191. Rom 2.5.

are three orders: *prophets* and *saints* and others *who fear the name* of
God. And consider whether catechumens are symbolized in piety
as *fearing the name* of God, but those *who* fear him and not just his
*name* are shown with the designation of *saints*. For, "Fear the Lord,
his saints, because they who fear him are not in want."[192] And it
seems[193] that you shall find *prophets* to be a kind of these *saints*. For
[the term] *saint* is broader than *prophet*. For necessarily the *prophet* of
God is also a *saint*, but the reverse is not [always so]. For there are
many *saints* who do not prophesy.

38.

Revelation 12.3–13.18a: (3) *And another sign was seen in heaven, and behold,*
*a great fiery dragon having seven heads and ten horns, and upon his heads were*
*seven diadems, (4) and his tail dragged down a third of the stars of heaven and*
*cast them upon the earth. And the dragon stood before the woman who was about*
*to give birth, so that when she gave birth he might devour her child. (5) And she*
*gave birth to a male son, who is destined to shepherd all nations with an iron*
*staff, and her child was taken up to God and to his throne. (6) And the woman*
*fled into the desert, where she has a place there prepared by God, so that there*
*they should nourish her one thousand two hundred sixty days. (7) And there was*
*war in heaven, Michael and his angels against the dragon. And the dragon and*
*his angels made war. (8) And they did not prevail, nor was there a place found*
*for them in heaven. (9) And the great dragon was cast down; the ancient serpent,*
*who is called the devil and Satan, the deceiver of the whole world, was cast down*
*upon the earth, and his angels were cast down with him. (10) And I heard a great*
*voice in heaven, saying, "Now is the salvation and the power and the kingdom*
*of our God and the authority of his Christ, because the accuser of our brethren*
*has been cast down, who accuses them before our God, day and night. (11) And*
*they conquered him by the blood of the Lamb and by the word of their testimony,*
*and they did not love their lives until death. (12) On account of this, rejoice,*
*heavens and those who dwell in them. Woe to the earth and to the sea because*
*the devil has descended to you, having great rage, seeing that he has little time."*
*(13) And when the dragon saw that he was cast upon the earth, he persecuted the*
*woman who gave birth to the male [child]. (14) And to the woman were given*
*two wings of a great eagle so that she might fly to the desert, to her place, so that*

192. Ps 33.10.
193. I follow Turner here, not Tzamalikos.

*there she might be nourished a time and times and half of a time from the face of the serpent. (15) And the serpent spewed water from his mouth like a river at the woman, so that he might make her to be carried away by the river. (16) And the earth helped the woman, and the earth opened its mouth and drank the river that the dragon had poured from his mouth. (17) And the dragon was enraged with the woman and departed to make war with the remainder of her seed, those who keep the commandments of God and have the testimony of Jesus. (18) And he stood upon the sand of the sea.*

*(13.1) And I saw a beast ascending from the sea; he had ten horns and seven heads, and upon his horns were ten diadems, and upon his heads were blasphemous names. (2) And the beast, which I saw, was similar to a leopard, and his feet were like those of a bear, and his mouth was like the mouth of lions. And the dragon gave to him his power and his throne and great authority. (3) And one of his heads was as if it was slain unto death. And the stroke of its death was healed, and all the earth was amazed before the beast. (4) And they worshiped the dragon because he gave authority to the beast. And they worshiped the beast, saying, "Who is like you, the beast, and who is able to make war against him?" (5) And a mouth was given to him to speak great things and blasphemy. And authority was given to him to make war for forty-two months. (6) And he opened his mouth to blaspheme God, to blaspheme his name and his dwelling, and [to blaspheme] those who dwell in heaven. (7) And it was granted to him to make war with the saints and to conquer them, and authority was given to him over every tribe and people and tongue and nation. (8) And all those who dwell upon the earth worshiped him,[194] the names of whom were not written in the book of life of the Lamb who was slain before the foundation of the world. (9) If anyone has ears, let him hear. (10) If anyone shall lead into captivity, he shall go into captivity. If anyone shall kill by the sword, it is necessary that he shall be killed by the sword. Here are the perseverance and the faith of the saints. (11) And I saw another beast rising from the earth, and he had two horns like a lamb, and he spoke as a dragon. (12) And he exercises all the authority of the first beast before him. And he makes the earth and those who dwell upon it to worship the first beast, whose stroke of death was healed. (13) And he works great signs, so that even fire from heaven descends to the earth before men. (14) And he deceives those who dwell upon the earth on account of the signs that are given to him to perform before the beast, saying that those who dwell upon the earth [must] make images of the beast, who sustained a stroke from a sword and lives. (15) And it was given to him to give a spirit*

194. Literally: "worship him."

*to the image of the beast, so that also the image of the beast might speak and make whoever did not worship the image of the beast to be killed.* (16) *And he makes everyone, the small and the great and the rich and the poor and the freedmen and the slaves, to receive*[195] *marks upon their right hands or upon their foreheads,* (17) *so that no one is even able to purchase or to sell unless he has the mark, the name of the beast or the number of his name.* (18a) *Here is*[196] *wisdom; he who has understanding, let him calculate the number of the beast. For it is the number of a man. His number ...*

[38A] *The dragon, who in an onslaught made war with the angels,* was crushed and *cast down* from heaven, and as he fell, he *dragged a third of the stars.* These particular *stars* are divine powers, like[197] those who apostatized with him and were brought down with the dragon. As Isaiah says, "How the Morningstar fell from heaven!"[198]

[38B from Irenaeus, *Against Heresies* 5.28.2–4, 29.1–2] *"And he stood upon the sand of the sea ..."* The Apostle says, "Because they did not receive the love of God so that they might be saved, and on account of this God sent to them an agent of deception so that they might believe the lie."[199] For when he has come and by his own purpose recapitulates unbelief in himself, and by his own free will does whatever he shall do and sits in the temple of God so that they who are deceived by him might worship him as Christ,[200] therefore indeed they shall justly be cast into the furnace of fire. But God, according to his own foreknowledge, having foreseen all things, at the appropriate time sends such a one who is destined to exist, so that they might believe the lie,[201] whose advent John has here disclosed in this way.[202] Therefore, so that one may not believe that he does signs by divine power, but by a magical agent, [John] said, *"And he deceives those who dwell upon the earth."* And no one ought to marvel that, if demons and apostate spirits serve him, he works

195. Literally: "so that he gives to them."
196. Literally: "has."
197. I follow Turner here, not Tzamalikos.
198. Is 14.12.
199. 2 Thes 2.10–11.
200. Cf. 2 Thes 2.4.
201. Cf. 2 Thes 2.11.
202. Here the scholiast skips much material in Irenaeus, and he does so even though it contains exegesis of the Apocalypse.

signs through them, by which he might deceive *those who dwell upon the earth*. But also [John] says the *number of his name* and that it is none other than the number *666*, which is six hundreds and six tens and six units, in order to recapitulate all the apostasy that has occurred over six thousand years. For in as many days as the world came to existence, in these are a thousand [years] completed. And on account of this, Scripture says, "And on the sixth day God completed his works which he did."[203] This is also a description of what would occur in the future, just as it happened, as well as a prophecy of what is still yet to be. For if a day of the Lord is as a thousand years,[204] but in six days what exists was completed, it is clear that the completion of them shall be in the six-thousandth year. And on account of this, in all of this time, man, who was formed in the beginning by the hands of God (that is, the Son and the Spirit), existed according to the image and likeness of God. Now chaff, which is abandoned, is [representative of] apostasy, but wheat, which is stored in the barn, is [representative of] those who bear fruit to God in faith.

And on account of this, persecution is also necessary for those who are saved, so that in a certain fashion, being winnowed and being kneaded through patience in the Word of God and being tested by fire, they might be fit for the feast of the kingdom, as a certain man of [bygone] days said, who was condemned to beasts on account of [his] testimony to God, "I am the grain of God, and through the teeth of beasts I am ground, so that I might be found as the pure bread of God."[205]

But we have shown the causes for this in previous books, by which God allowed this to be in this way. And we have shown that all such things are done on behalf of the man who is saved, maturing his free will for immortality and making him more suitable for eternal submission to God.

(And after other things:)[206] And on account of this, in the end,

---

203. Gn 2.2.

204. Cf. Ps 89.4; 2 Pt 3.8.

205. Ignatius of Antioch, *To the Romans* 4.1.

206. This phrase is present in the manuscript and shows that the scholiast is indicating that he is skipping from the beginning of section 5.29.1 of *Against Heresies* to the end of the same section.

when the Church shall be suddenly taken up from here, "There shall be," [Scripture] says, "tribulation such as has not been from the beginning nor shall be."[207] For this is the last contest of the righteous, in which, after they have conquered, they are crowned in immortality. And on account of this there shall be, in the [last] beast that comes, a recapitulation of all unrighteousness and every deception, so that, after all apostate power has flowed together in him, he might be cast into the furnace of fire. And so appropriately his *name* shall also have the *number 666*, recapitulating in himself the whole example of wickedness before the flood concerning the apostasy of the angels. For Noah was six hundred years old, and the flood came upon the earth, wiping away the high ground of the earth, on account of the adulterated generation of Adam. And recapitulating also ...

### 39.

Revelation 14.3b–5a:[208] (3b) ... *who were purchased from the earth.* (4) *These are they who were not defiled with women. For they are virgins. These are they who follow the Lamb wherever he goes. These were purchased by Jesus from among men as first fruits to God and to the Lamb.* (5a) *And in their mouth a lie is not found. For they are blameless.*

[From Irenaeus, *Against Heresies* 5.30.3] "*For the number of a man is 666.*"[209] It is safer and less dangerous to await the fulfillment of the prophecy than to guess and rave about names that present themselves, for many names can be found that have the aforementioned number. So this question cannot be solved. For if there are many names that are found possessing the number, it will be asked which of them the coming man shall bear. Because it is not on account of a lack of names ...[210]

---

207. Mt 24.21.

208. According to Harnack, Rv 14.1–3a is omitted in the manuscript.

209. Rv 13.18.

210. Irenaeus, *Against Heresies* 5.30.3. In the manuscript, the verso side of this folio is blank.

# INDICES

# GENERAL INDEX

Alulfus, 43
Ambrose Autpert, 43
Andrew of Caesarea, xviii, 7, 16, 85,
  100
Antichrist, xvii, 5–6, 9, 11, 14,
  27–29, 32, 34–35, 47–48, 52, 65,
  67, 76
Apollinaris of Laodicea, 13
Apringius of Beja, 13–14, 18, 22
Arethas of Caesarea, 85
Arian, 104, 112, 124, 128
Aristotle, 80
Augustine, 10, 12, 14, 18, 34–35, 48

Babylon, 9, 29, 31–33
Basil of Caesarea, 132
bishop, 8, 12, 19–21, 134

Caesarius of Arles, xviii
Cain, 52, 122
Cassian, John, 86, 94–95
Cassian the Sabaite, 86, 94–95
Chalcedonian, 48–49, 74
Clement of Alexandria, 7, 16, 85–86,
  93–94, 96, 99–100, 102, 110, 114
Constantinople, xviii, 3, 7, 13
cross, 9, 37, 74
crown, 19, 29–30, 57, 69, 127, 140, 149
Cyprian of Carthage, 29
Cyril of Alexandria, 86, 95, 103, 119

Didymus the Blind, 85, 93–94,
  96–105, 107, 109, 111, 114, 116–17,
  119, 121–24, 128, 130, 132, 136–37,
  144
Domitian, emperor, 7

earthquake, 5, 31
ecclesiology, 12, 44, 47, 50, 76
elect, 44–45, 48, 59, 64, 69, 75
Elijah, 6, 9, 27, 48, 64, 126
Elisha, 50
end of the world, 5–6, 9, 14, 16, 24, 27,
  30, 32, 34, 47–48, 60, 63, 66
Enoch, 6, 9, 27, 48
Epiphanius of Salamis, 16
*Epistle of Barnabas,* 22
eschatology, 44, 47, 87
Eucherius of Lyons, 31
Eusebius of Caesarea, 98

figure, 5, 22, 44–46, 50, 63–64
Filastrius of Brixia, 13

Gabriel, the archangel, 66
garment, 21, 55, 72, 74. *See also* robe
Gnostic, 103, 119
Gog and Magog, 5, 35
grace, 48, 50, 57, 61

heaven, 5, 9, 11, 21, 23, 25, 27, 29–30,
  33, 44–48, 61–62, 65–66, 69–71, 73,
  75–76, 78–79, 126, 129
hell, 18, 35–37, 70, 115
Heracleon, the Valentinian, 103,
  119
heretics, 116–18
Hesychius of Dalmatia, 13
Hippolytus, xviii, 22, 86, 95
Holy Spirit, 6, 20, 23, 35, 47, 50–51,
  112, 114, 120, 124–27, 148
homoians, 7
hypocrites, 12, 65

iconoclasm, 89
Ignatius of Antioch, 148
interpretation: Alexandrian, 89;
    allegorical, 5, 24, 41, 100; anagogi-
    cal, 111, 116; figurative, 44–46, 50,
    63–64; grammatical, 43–46, 133;
    historical, 41, 87, 116; literal, 32, 44,
    87; moral, 41; mystical, 5, 17, 30, 87;
    physical, 87, 136; spiritual, 8, 19,
    44, 87, 117, 136; supra-sensible, 126,
    128, 136; symbolic, 113; synecdoche,
    9, 12, 34–35
Irenaeus of Lyons, 16, 18, 22, 87, 94,
    96, 99, 106, 147, 149
Islam, 90

Jerome, 10, 12, 34–35, 92, 98
Jerusalem, 9, 12, 35–36, 70, 121–23
Jesus Christ: Ascension, 51, 112,
    129; deity/divinity, 18, 56, 73, 104,
    123–24, 127–28; Incarnation, 12–13,
    46, 49, 51, 73, 75, 81, 112, 121, 131;
    Nativity, 9, 34; Passion, 9, 37, 56,
    74, 111–12, 129, 131; Second Com-
    ing, 5–6, 9, 12–14, 17–18, 29, 36–37,
    78; unity, 49, 110
John, 7–9, 15–18, 21, 31, 33, 36–37, 46,
    50, 53, 57–60, 63–66, 68–70, 72–74,
    79–82, 85, 90, 93, 101, 108–9, 118,
    126, 136, 143; John the Theologian,
    89, 101–2, 107, 109, 112
Judas (Iscariot), 52
judgment, 5, 9, 11, 19–21, 29, 46–48,
    56–58, 64, 69–70, 78, 88, 128–29,
    134, 144

Leviathan, 48, 72, 75

martyrs, 24, 29–31, 35, 116, 138
Mary, 9, 13, 27, 57; Virgin, 48, 74–75, 81
Methodius of Olympus, 98
Michael, the archangel, 9, 13, 27, 48,
    66–67, 145
monophysitism, 89
monothelitism, 89–90
mysteries, 4–5, 17–18, 36, 51, 141

Neophytus the Recluse, 85
Nestorius, 74

Oecumenius, xviii, 7, 16, 85, 89, 100
Origen, 85, 89–94, 96–105, 107–9,
    111–12, 114–23, 125–26, 129–32,
    134–35, 137, 143–44
Ostrogoths, 3, 7

paradise, 19
Paterius, 42–43
Philo of Alexandria, 106, 138
Philocalia, 99
preachers, 17, 19, 48, 51, 55, 60, 63–64,
    67, 81
Primasius of Hadrumetum, xviii, 6,
    10–12, 14, 17–19, 22, 30, 32–37
Procopius of Gaza, 98
punishment, 6, 19, 29, 71, 115, 133

Quodvultdeus of Carthage, 13

Raphael, the archangel, 16, 66
reprobate, 48, 52, 60, 66–67
resurrection, 5, 8–9, 11–12, 18, 19, 35,
    49, 56, 58–60, 77, 81
robe, 8, 17, 24, 30, 33, 48, 60, 74, 109,
    137–38, 140. See also garment

Simon (Magus), 52
Simplicius, 120

Theodoret of Cyrus, 102, 111, 132
thousand years, 10–13, 34–35, 47,
    75–77, 148
Trinity, 7, 15, 31
Tyconius, xvii–xviii, 4–5, 10, 12, 14–15,
    19–20, 22, 24, 26–27, 30, 32–35,
    37, 49

Victorinus of Petovium, xvii, 6, 10–12,
    14, 17, 20, 22, 32, 49
Vigilius of Thapse, 10–11, 13–14

# INDEX OF HOLY SCRIPTURE

*New Testament*